Developing an Effective Run Game With Zone and Gap Schemes

John Rose

ISBN: 978-1-60679-205-6
Library of Congress Control Number: 2012930084
Cover design: Studio J Art & Design
Book layout: Studio J Art & Design
Diagrams: John Rice
Front cover photo: ©Troy Wayryen/NewSport/ZUMAPRESS.com

Coaches Choice
P.O. Box 1828
Monterey, CA 93942
www.coacheschoice.com

Dedication

To my wife, Lois, who put up with my physical absence when I was at coaching meetings, coaching clinics, practice, and games and my mental absence when I was thinking about football when I should have been listening to her.

Also, to my two adult children, Lauri and Ed, who grew up watching their father waste reams of paper diagramming plays.

To all the fine coaches I've worked with over the years, especially Dick Bergstrom, the head coach at Creston Orient-Macksburg High School, under whom I served for 30 years. Dick always allowed his coaches to coach, and without his leadership, I truly would have never coached as long as I did.

Finally, to all the players I coached over the years at Adair-Casey High School and Creston O-M High School. I have the greatest respect for each and every one of you—from those who started to those who were reserves—even though I didn't express those feelings enough.

Contents

Introduction

My coaching career began in the fall of 1970 as the offensive line coach at Adair-Casey High School in Adair, Iowa. I was to spend the next six seasons there, serving under two head coaches and two offensive systems: the full house T belly series at first and then a pro set featuring split backs and the I formation.

At that time, offensive linemen were prohibited from extending their hands, which made pass blocking difficult at best. Run offense still dominated, with the use of several blocking schemes based on the backfield action. Adair-Casey ran dive plays with man blocking, isolation plays with double-teams, power off-tackle plays, middle trap plays, and the power sweep, which became our feature play.

Each scheme required its own set of blocking rules, which required offensive linemen to memorize sets of priorities, such as on, over, inside, etc. Some very good coaches at the time would vary the scheme based on the defensive alignment, so linemen had to memorize a scheme versus, for example, a 5-2 or versus a 4-4. That worked at a time when the defensive fronts that a team was likely to encounter were limited. Rarely would you encounter more than two alignments in any single game.

In 1976, I accepted a job as assistant football coach at a larger school: Creston High School in Creston, Iowa. Between 1977 and 1983, the head coach, Dick Bergstrom, employed a variety of offenses, including the split back veer, power-T, slot-I, and wing-T. The constant between all these systems was that they involved complicated blocking rules specific to each play.

By 1984, the Creston staff made the decision to return to the veer offense, featuring the inside veer and outside veer. By this time, offensive linemen were allowed to extend their hands for pass blocking; later, they were allowed to use their hands during run plays too. An improved passing game combined with the veer option contributed to a breakthrough season in 1985 at a school, which, quite frankly, was hardly known for football success. For the first time, Creston qualified for the playoffs.

That season seemed to be the springboard for future success, with the option game and an ever-improving passing game being the constants in Creston's offensive approach. By 1989, players from Orient-Macksburg High School joined Creston High School players to create the Creston O-M Panthers. The offense changed to the pro I formation but continued to emphasize the option, supplemented with power, the trap, the toss sweep, and the counter gap.

Because Creston O-M did not platoon offense and defense, practicing pass protection schemes, along with at least five run block schemes in one practice per week became a burden. Mondays were for films and junior varsity games. Tuesdays were the offensive practice, Wednesday for defense, and Thursdays the dress rehearsal. It began to become apparent that the number of blocking schemes was having an adverse affect on blocking fundamentals.

By the mid 1990s, the coaching staff began to become interested in a new trend in college and pro football: zone blocking. The appeal that zone blocking held was that it was a way to run inside and outside with one blocking scheme. On the surface, all an offensive lineman needed to know was whether he was covered or uncovered. The other appeal of zone blocking was that it enabled greater depth. If the sixth-best interior lineman was a tackle, he could also be a guard because of the consistency in rules and techniques at all positions.

After listening to a presentation at a football clinic by University of Nebraska offensive line coach Milt Tenopir on blending the zone scheme with the option, our staff set up a visit with him at the Nebraska football facilities. He graciously spent the entire day with us and sent us on our way with an invaluable instructional video. As a result, Creston O-M installed inside zone blocking for the fullback dive as well as for interior tailback plays. At that time, the approach to outside zone blocking was to have the covered lineman attempt to escape to linebacker level, with the uncovered man attempting to overtake the defensive lineman. Creston O-M used that approach for the option play as well as the tailback pitch sweep.

However, after one season, the decision was made to drop outside zone blocking for our outside plays and go back to reach blocking, with pulling linemen for our pitch sweep play. Inside zone blocking remained as the foundation for the inside game and was also adapted to the option plays. Although the outside and inside zone schemes were the same, the techniques for the outside zone were difficult to become proficient in. Creston O-M ran the trap, power, and counter gap schemes, along with the inside zone and all the pass protection schemes. In retrospect, the practice time required to execute so many schemes was responsible for the failure to execute outside zone blocking.

By the end of the 1990s, Creston O-M's approach remained much the same, although becoming more multiple, incorporating more one-back and shotgun formations, and running as much of the run offense as possible from all of them. However, strong trends were emerging in the collegiate and pro games. It seemed that with more and more emphasis on the passing game, the run games were becoming simpler. At that time, our staff had the privilege of visiting with Steve Loney, who was the offensive coordinator and offensive line coach at Iowa State University. Loney made a point that was eventually to become central to Creston O-M's offensive philosophy. With the unavoidable risks involved in protecting the passer, pro and collegiate offensive coaches were excluding run plays that were more likely to lose yards and get an offense off schedule. Offensive coordinators had to live with quarterback sacks, but they were no longer willing to accept bad plays in the run game. In Loney's opinion, the zone was the run play that was least likely to result in a loss.

Also, at about this time, the Denver Broncos were running a version of the outside zone that was being referred to by television commentators as the Bronco cutback zone. Our staff purchased a video presentation from Gilman Gear titled *Alex Gibbs Outside Zone*. The video featured a clinic lecture by Alex Gibbs, the Broncos' offensive line coach. The simplicity of the technique when compared to the older escape and overtake outside zone techniques became a revelation.

As Gibbs explained, the Broncos emphasized only two run plays: tight zone and wide zone. However, the difference was that they weren't really trying to get the ball outside on the outside zone play. The technique of the uncovered lineman wasn't to overtake. Instead, the uncovered man's technique was to push the defensive lineman to the outside and into the reach block of the covered lineman before he, the uncovered man, popped up on the linebacker. That technique, combined with the strict discipline of the Denver running backs, was the reason for the success of the Bronco run game at that time. The Bronco running backs were coached to key the block on the defensive end and make one vertical cut if they couldn't get outside, which, because of the blocking technique, was usually the case. We also visited with members of the University of Iowa staff, who had used a similar approach in their run game to help them win a Big Ten championship in 2002.

As the Creston O-M offense became more multiple, with different personnel packages, ranging from four wide receivers to two backs and two tight ends, the decision was made to simplify the run game to only two run block schemes. By 2005 Creston O-M was running the outside zone and inside zone by using the Denver Broncos' wide zone technique, with minor variations, as the basis for both plays.

To supplement the zone scheme, the gap scheme was retained because power gap is a good change-up to the zone, especially in short-yardage situations. The gap scheme in the form of counter gap is also the perfect counter to zone blocking because the down blocks of the offensive linemen resemble zone blocking going in the opposite direction to defenders.

Over a period of 35 years coaching the offensive line at two schools, I came to develop the following offensive philosophies:
- When designing the run offense, avoid the mindset of running plays. Instead, think in terms of running blocking schemes and then adapt the plays to the schemes. Select blocking schemes you can practice and execute, and run several plays from the same scheme(s). If a play can't be adapted to the schemes that you use, don't run the play. Less is more!
- Communication is key. A coach must be very careful about the words he chooses to use when he teaches a technique or scheme. Once an impression is made in the mind of a player, a coach can't easily remove it.

- Everything that's done in practice must be specific to the scheme. A coach doesn't even have as much as one second to waste once two-a-days begin in August. Drills for the sake of doing drills are a total waste of time. Drills that teach or reinforce the scheme are optimal.
- All schemes and fundamentals that relate to them must be thoroughly taught and understood by the players during two-a-day drills. Teams won't have time for these drills once the game week routines begin.
- Game week is for adopting what has been learned about the opponent, and experimentation and/or additions are to be avoided.
- As much as possible, all players should have an understanding of the whole scheme, not just their role in it. When players understand the reasons behind what they do and understand the role of others, they can better adjust to what's happening on the field.
- Multiple formations and motions should be used versus every opponent to create advantages in the run game when the defense adjusts to the formation. It's not necessary to run every play out of every formation but rather to choose a few runs out of a few formations that create defensive problems against specific opponent.
- A strong three-step drop pass offense is mandatory if you use a multiple formation attack. When a defense refuses to align a defender on a slot receiver, that means they have too many in the box versus the run and the offense must have a way to make them pay.
- A strong play-action pass game, including misdirection passes, must be part of any run offense for obvious reasons. The more a defense has to worry about the pass, the less players they can commit to the run.
- An option play should be a part of every run offense. A defense must be forced to be sound versus the option or else they'll be able to overload versus some formations. As an example, if a defense rotates to a three-deep coverage versus trips and slides all the linebackers to the trips side, there would be no defender assigned to the pitchback on the weakside. The threat of the option limits the adjustment that a defense can make and therefore opens advantages to the offense in the adjustments that are made.

This book is about developing a system of offensive line plays for the high school run game. Although these plays are specific to a system developed and used by one high school over a period of years, I'm not in any way claiming that it's superior to any other system.

Above all, a coach is a teacher, and it's always best to coach what you can teach and what you believe in. The only limitation on any blocking system should be what can be taught and what can be practiced in the time that's available. It's better to do a good job of teaching too little, rather than teaching too much and risking poor execution as a result.

The one concept that's more important than any other is the concept of structuring the run game around the blocking schemes rather than the plays that are run. Because players benefit most from continuity, the selected schemes should be sustainable. Sustainability means that the schemes can be used for a variety of plays should a change in offenses become necessary. Sustainability also means that if other schemes are added or substituted that the new concepts and skills be related to the already learned concepts and skills as much as possible.

As a coach, I always tried to learn as much as possible about the schemes and techniques other coaches taught. I attended as many clinics as possible and bought innumerable books, manuals, and video presentations. What I learned early on was that it's futile to copy but that it's invaluable to adapt. That's what I would hope could be gained by reading this book. If just one idea benefits the reader, then this book is a success.

1

The Evolution of Zone Blocking

In 1970, college football was just beginning to employ wide receivers on a regular basis, with various forms of the option offense indicating a strong future trend. In the middle 1960s, the NCAA had legislated free substitution, which allowed for platoon football. Prior to that, college offenses generally consisted of two tight end types and two running back types at the halfback positions. When or if wide receivers were employed, one of the ends and/or one of the halfbacks would split wide. In addition, all offensive players had to be proficient at a defensive position.

Free substitution not only led to the development of offensive and defensive specializations, but it also enabled offensive coaches to build offenses that could employ receiving specialists. College football began imitating professional football, with high schools not far behind. When offenses consistently began to split one end and one back, that left one less blocker at the line of scrimmage and one less back to fake to or be used as a lead blocker. With the exception of wishbone triple option teams or Delaware wing-T teams, college running games were now structured around two backs: a fullback and a tailback.

The most predominant defensive alignment of the time was so popular that it was often referred to as the "NCAA defense." The 52 slant created problems to the man block schemes of that time. Offensive linemen who were assigned to fire out and block a specific defender couldn't prevent a slanting lineman from controlling a gap. The result was that ballcarriers were forced to alter their course and encounter unblocked linebackers who had moved opposite the slant. These problems could be overcome from two back formations if one of the two backs were employed as a lead blocker.

Figure 1-1 illustrates an isolation play versus a 52. If the defensive tackle slanted inside, the fullback could read the slant and block one gap wider on the scraping backer, with the tailback following his block.

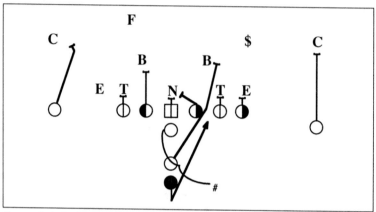

Figure 1-1. Isolation play vs. 52

However, using one back as a blocker in a two-back formation all but eliminated deception. In older three-back formations, one back could be a blocker, one back could be a faker, and one back could carry the ball. The increasing popularity of option football in the 1970s, combined with two-back and two wide receiver formations, meant that the inside threat of a dive option wouldn't have a lead blocker. Slanting linemen made it difficult to establish the man block dive play.

Figure 1-2 illustrates how a dive back would be forced wider by an inside slant into the unblocked scraping linebacker. If the play had been run to the other side, the ballcarrier would have been tackled by the slanting noseguard.

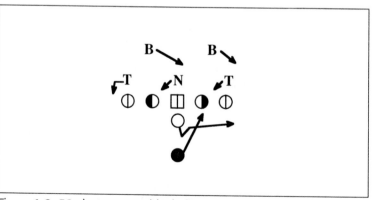

Figure 1-2. 52 slant vs. man block dive

Whether run from split backs, the I formation, or the three-back wishbone, the triple option came about in large part because of the challenge represented by the 52 slant. Leaving the defender who's aligned on the playside tackle unblocked enabled the tackle to block the playside backer and the guard to double-team the noseguard. This blocking scheme, combined with a quarterback read to determine a hand off or a keep, meant that the slanting defensive tackle would always be wrong.

Figure 1-3 illustrates the triple option versus the 52 alignment. If the defensive tackle slanted to the inside, he would be checked by the tackle's inside release. The quarterback would disconnect and the fullback would block the scraping playside backer. The quarterback and tailback would then execute the option on the defensive end. If the defensive tackle didn't move to the inside or slanted outside, the ball would be handed off to the fullback, who would be able to veer outside the double-team block of the guard and center on the noseguard and the seal block of the tackle on the playside backer.

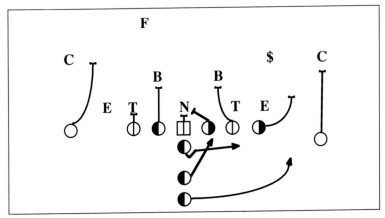

Figure 1-3. Triple option vs. 52

The problem with the triple option was that the amount of practice time that had to be devoted to it detracted from pass offense execution. Most offensive coaches of the 1970s and 1980s who wanted to incorporate option football chose to predetermine the dive and the option so they could maintain a more balanced approach to offense. The solutions they found to the dive problem were the forerunners of the modern zone scheme.

The problem of the slanting noseguard and scraping backside backer was solved with a type of slant read in which the center and backside guard would step into their playside gaps and read the slant as they stepped. If the noseguard played straight or slanted playside, the center would block him and the guard would block the backside backer. If the nose slanted backside, the center would block the scraping backer and the guard would block the slanting noseguard (Figure 1-4).

The slant read that sealed the backside led to a type of cutback dive in which the playside guard would step into his outside gap before climbing for the backer. An inside slant by the defensive tackle would result in a double-team between the guard and tackle, with the backer scraping to the outside being unblocked. The back would now cut back under the double-team and scraping backer. If the back encountered a playside slant by the noseguard, he would cut behind the center's block on the slanting nose. Figure 1-5 illustrates the fullback dive with these adjustments.

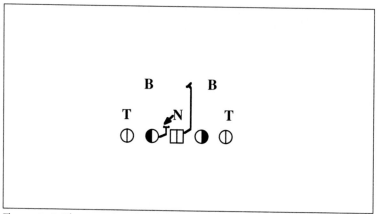

Figure 1-4. Slant read vs. backside slant

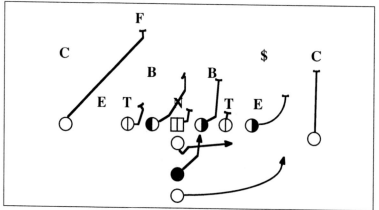

Figure 1-5. Dive vs. 52

Although these approaches resembled zone blocking, they weren't true zone because they weren't coordinated into an across-the-board system. Instead, they were components of other schemes, which were used to solve specific problems presented by specific defenses. A true zone system emphasizes zone combos against all defensive alignments.

The development of the true zone is closely related to the adoption of the one back and three wide receiver formations by a number of college and pro teams in the 1980s and 1990s. A one-back formation has no lead blocker, and the ballcarrier is aligned in a much deeper position so he can threaten inside and outside simultaneously. In addition, defenses now began overshifting to the tight end side, which had the effect of protecting linebackers by stacking them behind defensive linemen. Across-the-board zone combos were developed to account for stacked linebackers and to allow a deep tailback to find the bubble caused by defensive alignment or by defensive movement (Figure 1-6).

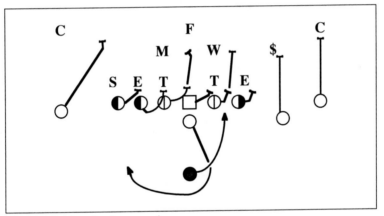

Figure 1-6. One-back zone play

A one-back sequence evolved in which a back's initial movement for the inside run and the outside run looked the same—thus, the inside and outside zones. These plays, coupled with a counter and a draw, became a minimalist run game, which in turn meant more practice time for the passing game.

Of course, any blocking system that can be used by one-back formations can also be used by two-back formations. Multiple-formation teams who wanted a set of plays that could be run from one-back and two-back formations began to abandon the fullback run game so they could feature the tailback zone plays. The fullback, or H-back as he was called by some coaches, became a blocker and receiver only.

Figure 1-7 illustrates an inside zone play from a two-back formation in which the fullback blocks to the backside to ensure a possible cutback. Figure 1-8 illustrates an outside zone play in which the fullback serves as a lead blocker. The tailback aims for the tight end's rear end and runs outside his block or makes one vertical cut inside.

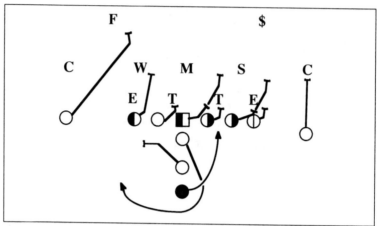

Figure 1-7. Inside zone

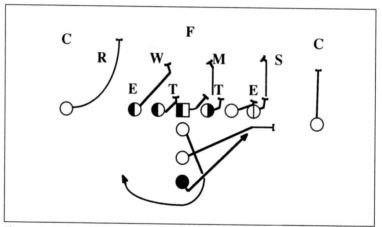

Figure 1-8. Outside zone

2

Terminology

Eighty percent of the mystery about football to those who don't follow the game closely is terminology. Even more confusing is that football coaches often have different names for the same thing. Therefore, it's essential that a coaching staff agree on terminology and that they're very careful not to deviate from that on the practice field or in the meeting room.

Every offense has a way of communicating which of its several plays it wishes to execute. Dozens, if not hundreds, of ways have been used. Some coaches simply name their plays. Others use a numbering system. Perhaps the most common is to number all possible ballcarriers and then number the points of attack along the offensive line. A two-digit number designates the ballcarrier with the first number and the point of attack with the second.

Yet another system applies the first digit to the series or the type of sequence being run in the backfield. For example, in the split back veer, if the teen series is the veer option series, then 12 may be the dive play to the right and 13 the dive play to the left. It's the halfback's responsibility to know that he carries the ball on 12 and left halfback's responsibility to fake the option to the right. Conversely, it's the left halfback's responsibility to know that he carries the ball on 13 and the right halfback's responsibility to fake the option to the left. Obviously, the second digit is still the point of attack.

In yet another system, a three-digit number is used. The first digit is the formation, the second is either the ballcarrier or the series, and the third is the point of attack. Whichever numbering system is used, attaching a word or words to the end of the number to designate the type of play or the blocking scheme is very common. Because every coach has his own system, the run plays described in this book are referred to by name rather than by number.

The run plays featured in this book, along with their blocking schemes, are as follows:

- Wide zone (zone)
- Tight zone (zone)
- Option (zone)
- Power (gap)
- Counter (gap)

When teaching players who they should block, a coach must have a system of referring to defensive players. Probably the most universal system is the one that's been attributed to the legendary Paul "Bear" Bryant. Numbers are assigned to possible defensive alignments, which are referred to as *techniques*. The alignments of each technique are as follows:

- If a defensive lineman is aligned head-up, he's given an even number. A 0 technique is on the center, a 2 technique is on the guard, a 4 technique is on the tackle, a 6 technique is on the tight end, and an 8 technique is on a wide defensive player aligned outside the box.
- A defensive lineman who's aligned in an outside shade is given an odd number. A 1 technique is a shade on the center, a 3 technique is an outside shade on the guard, a 5 technique is an outside shade on the tackle, and a 9 technique is an outside shade on the tight end.
- An inside shade on the guard is a 2i, an inside shade on the tackle is a 4i, and an inside shade on the tight end is a 7 technique.
- When referring to linebackers, a 0 is added to the end of the number. For example, a backer in an outside shade on the guard is a 30 technique.

Zone blocking requires defensive gaps because zone blocking is about blocking any defender who's responsible for a particular gap. Defensive gaps are as follows:

- The center–guard gap is the A gap.
- The guard–tackle gap is the B gap.
- The tackle–tight end gap is the C gap.
- The area to the outside of the tight end is the D gap.

The terms *playside* and *backside* are familiar to most football coaches. Playside refers to the side of the offensive line that a play is directed at and backside refers to the side away from the point of attack. The areas of responsibility for all offensive linemen in zone scheme are as follows:

- *Backside tight end*: Backside C gap
- *Backside tackle:* Backside B gap
- *Backside guard:* Backside A gap
- *Center:* Playside A gap
- *Playside guard:* Playside B gap
- *Playside tackle:* Playside C gap
- *Playside tight end:* Playside D gap

The concept of the box must also be understood by all players. Defenders can be referred to as being in the box or out of the box. The box is an imaginary area extending from the outside shoulder of the tight end on one side to the outside shoulder of the tight end (or imaginary tight end) on the other side—to a depth of 5 yards.

Although it's best to refer to defensive linemen by technique, a coach should name certain defensive positions or alignments for teaching purposes:

- *Defensive end:* When a team runs the option to the split end side, the defensive end is defined as the last defender who's on the line of scrimmage, regardless of whether he's a backer or defensive back. If he's on the line, he's the defensive end.
- *Mike linebacker:* The linebacker who plays over the center or the first playside backer if no true middle backer exists.
- *Buck linebacker:* The second middle backer in 30 defenses.
- *Sam linebacker:* The linebacker who aligns to the tight end side.
- *Will linebacker:* The linebacker who aligns to the split end side.
- *Rover:* The outside linebacker in eight-man fronts who aligns on the split end side.
- *Cornerback:* The defensive back who's the farthest to the outside.
- *Safety:* The defensive back (or backs) who aligns between the two cornerbacks.
- *The force player:* An outside linebacker or defensive back who's responsible for run contain, which includes being responsible for the pitch versus the option.
- A specific defensive alignment is referred to by a two-digit number; the first digit refers to the number of linemen and the second refers to the number of linebackers. A descriptive name can also be attached. Examples: 43 over or 33 stack.

In a multiple offense that achieves its multiplicity by substitution, sideline communication is critical. The easiest method of designating who should be in the game is to name each personnel group and communicate it by voice or flash card and then to signal the exact formation once the proper players are on the field. The following are some ways personnel groups could be named:

- *Black:* One tight end, one fullback, one tailback, and two wide receivers. If the word Jet is attached, that means a second tailback will replace the fullback.
- *White:* One fullback, one tailback, and three wide receivers.
- *Orange:* Two tight ends, one fullback, one tailback, and one wide receiver.
- *Red:* Two tight ends, two fullbacks, and one tailback.
- *Green:* Two tight ends, one tailback, and two wide receivers.
- *Gold:* One tight end, one tailback, and three wide receivers.
- *Blue:* One tailback and four wide receivers.

Once the proper personnel are on the field, their alignment can be signaled to the quarterback by the following names:

- *Right/Left (Black):* A conventional two-back pro-I formation, with a tight end and flanker on the strongside and a split end on the weakside (Figure 2-1). In the orange and red groups, a second tight end would replace the split end. In red, a second fullback would also replace the flanker and align as a halfback on the strongside.
- *Twins (Black):* A two-back I formation, with the two wide receivers on the strongside and the tight end on the weakside (Figure 2-2). In white, a third wide receiver would replace the tight end.
- *Ace (Green):* A two-tight-end-and-one-back formation, with one wide receiver on each side (Figure 2-3).

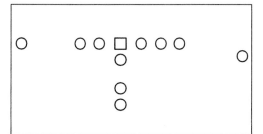

Figure 2-1. Right

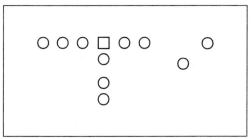

Figure 2-2. Twins right

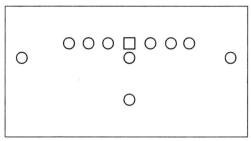

Figure 2-3. Ace right

- *Space (Gold):* A one tight end and one-back formation, with one wide receiver on the tight end side and twin wide receivers on the other side (Figure 2-4).
- *Trips (Gold):* A one tight end and one-back formation, with two wide receivers on the tight end side and one wide receiver on the weakside (Figure 2-5). In the green group, a second tight end would replace the weakside receiver.
- *Quads (Blue):* A one-back formation, with two wide receivers on each side (Figure 2-6).
- *Spread (Blue):* A one-back formation, with three wide receivers on the strongside and one wide receiver on the weakside (Figure 2-7). In gold, a tight end would replace the weakside receiver.

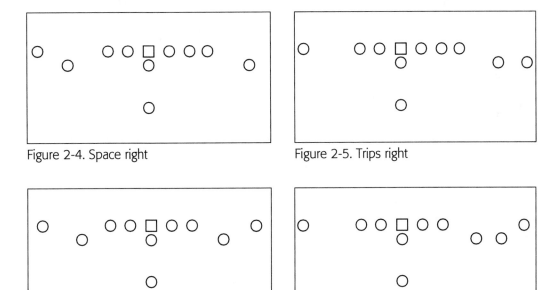

Figure 2-4. Space right

Figure 2-5. Trips right

Figure 2-6. Quads right

Figure 2-7. Spread right

In addition, the following words can be applied to personnel groups and/or formations:

- *Gun:* Can be applied to any formation; it aligns the quarterback in the shotgun, with the tailback aligned as a halfback to either side depending on the play or pass protection called. In black or white, the tailback would align weak and the fullback would align strong (Figure 2-8).

- *Wing/Slot:* Can be applied to any two-back formation; it tells the fullback to align as a wingback 1 yard outside the end man in the box. *Wing* means align on the tight end side and *slot* means line up on the split end side (Figure 2-9). In red, the second fullback would align as the wing.

- *Flex:* Can be applied to any tight end formation; it tells the tight end to split wide (Figure 2-10).

- *X:* Can be applied to any tight end formation; it tells the tight end to align off the line of scrimmage and the wide receiver to that side to align on the line (Figure 2-11).

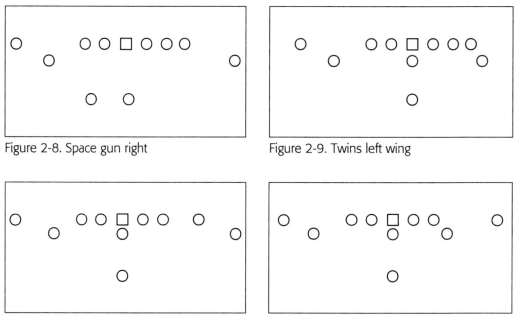

Figure 2-8. Space gun right

Figure 2-9. Twins left wing

Figure 2-10. Space right flex

Figure 2-11. Space right X

Communication

An essential element for any system of run blocking is a method of communicating to the blockers—that is, who they should block. This can be done by requiring the players to memorize rules, which are usually based on priorities, such as on, inside, outside, over, etc. It can also be done by making blocking calls at the line of scrimmage. Many different methods exist, whether it be the quarterback, center, uncovered lineman, etc., making the calls.

The appeal of zone blocking is that it eliminates complicated blocking rules. In theory, all a lineman needs to know is whether he's covered or uncovered. A covered lineman is one who has a defensive lineman aligned on any part of his body, whether it's head-up, inside shade, or outside shade. An uncovered lineman is one who has no defensive lineman aligned on him.

For example, in the inside zone, a covered man will block the playside number of the man on him and the uncovered man will block the backside number. Depending on whether the defensive lineman slants inside, one of the two offensive linemen would end up on the linebacker. The only exception is the backside tackle, who determines if the backside guard is covered, in which case he's obligated to help the guard.

Although the covered/uncovered approach seems simple and easy to understand, when coaching players, nothing is simple. The problem is that when confronted with shaded defenders, too many opportunities for misinterpretation occur. For example, a guard who's covered by a wide 3 technique might assume he's uncovered or a tight end might assume that a 5 technique on a tackle is in fact a 7 technique on him. What results are too many answers and too many excuses because the coach can't be on the field to explain it to the players.

As a result, a team should use a system of calls to determine who to block. Some coaches prefer to have the center make front calls, which determine specific zone combos, but this places too much of a burden on a player who has to deal with the snap count. Other coaches place that responsibility on the quarterback, but once again, that's too much for a player who has to read coverages and may have to audible plays.

The blocking system described in this book is based on calls made by the playside and backside guards:
- The two guards make calls based on their perceptions of the defensive look in their area. They're never wrong; the team will execute the calls that are made.
- The playside guard controls the playside call, with the tackle controlling the tight end if he's uncovered. The playside calls are based on whether the man making the call is covered or uncovered.
- The backside guard controls the backside call—again, with the tackle controlling the backside tight end against a very specific backside look. The backside guard's calls are based on a priority of the defensive tackle's technique.
- The players are coached to make the proper calls, but the bottom line is that it's their perception and that their call will be executed by everyone. This eliminates confusion about who a gap defensive player is shaded on.

In a system of calls, any name can be used, including the first name of the player that the caller wants to effect. This system uses names that are somewhat descriptive of the players involved. As an example, a *tag* call means tackle and guard. When a call is made, the uncovered man must call out the number of the backer that the combo is going to.

Cage (Figure 3-1): The playside guard will call *cage* to the center when the guard is covered. Cage means that the center and guard will combo the man on the guard to the Mike or first playside backer. A 1 technique on the center isn't considered covered by the guard, but if he makes the call versus the 1 technique, they'll execute it.

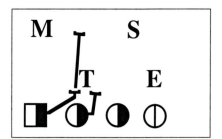
Figure 3-1. Cage

Tag (Figure 3-2): The playside guard will call *tag* to the tackle when the guard is uncovered. Tag means that the guard and tackle will combo the man on the tackle to the first playside backer. If the guard perceives that a 3 technique is a 4i technique and calls tag, they'll execute the call.

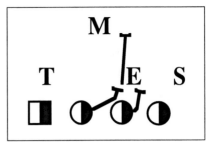

Figure 3-2. Tag

Zorro (Figure 3-3): Whenever the playside guard is double-gapped, with a headgear in the A gap and the B gap, he'll call *Zorro* to the center and tackle. Zorro means true zone; the center will block the A gap defender, the guard the B gap defender, the tackle the C gap defender, and the tight end the D gap.

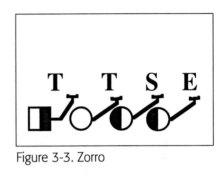

Figure 3-3. Zorro

Ted (Figure 3-4): When the tackle is unaffected by the guard's call, he must determine if he's covered or uncovered. If he's covered by a 5 technique, he should call out that technique to the tight end so the tight end knows he's covered by the next man outside the 5 technique. If the tackle is uncovered, he calls *Ted* to the tight end. Ted means the tackle and tight end will combo the man on the tight end to the second playside backer, counting from the Mike backer.

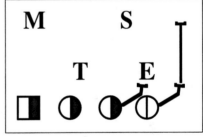

Figure 3-4. Ted

Fire (Figure 3-5): When the tight end gets a Ted call from the tackle, he'll call *fire* to the tackle when the second playside backer aligns on the line of scrimmage, as in a fire stunt. Fire tells the tackle to block the man on the tight end alone while the tight end blocks out on the backer.

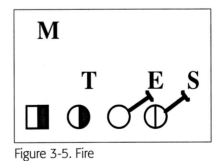

Figure 3-5. Fire

Wide (Figure 3-6): When the tight end gets a Ted call from the tackle, he'll call *wide* to the tackle when the man on him is a wide 9 technique. Wide tells the tackle to lateral step through the C gap to the Sam backer while the tight end blocks the wide 9 technique alone.

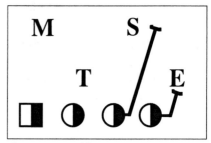
Figure 3-6. Wide

Tex (Figure 3-7): When the word *option* or *force* is part of the huddle call, the tackle will call *Tex* instead of Ted when he's uncovered. Tex means the tackle and tight end will combo the man on the tight end to the first backer in the box, counting from outside/in. Tex also tells the cage combo they can combo to the backside backer.

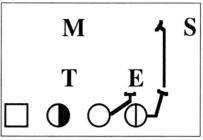
Figure 3-7. Tex

Center's rule (Figure 3-8): The center will block a 0 or playside 1 technique. The center will regard a backside 1 technique as uncovered and will therefore respond to the playside guard's *cage* call. If the center doesn't get a call, he'll block through the playside A gap to the most dangerous backer.

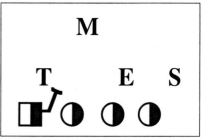
Figure 3-8. Center's rule

Eagle (Figure 3-9): When the center and the playside guard are both covered, the center will call *Eagle.* He'll then execute the cage call. The backside guard will block the 0 technique and the backside tackle will block the backside guard's area. In effect, an Eagle call creates a four-man zone.

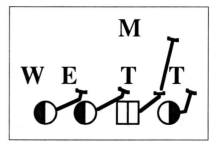
Figure 3-9. Eagle

Smash (Figure 3-10): *Smash* will be called by the backside guard when a 0 technique is played on the center. Smash means that the guard and the center will scoop combo the 0 technique to the Mike or backside backer.

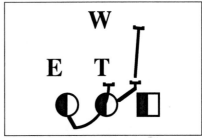

Figure 3-10. Smash

Uno (Figure 3-11): *Uno* will be called by the backside guard versus a backside 1 technique. Uno tells the backside tackle that the guard will block the 1 technique and that the tackle will block through the B gap to the backside backer. If a lineman should be in the B gap, the tackle will block him.

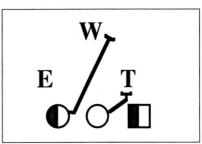

Figure 3-11. Uno

Banjo (Figure 3-12): *Banjo* will be called by the backside guard when he's covered and there is no 0 technique. Banjo means that the tackle and guard will scoop combo the man on the guard to the backside backer.

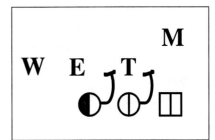

Figure 3-12. Banjo

Take it (Figure 3-13): If no backside backer exists, the tackle will respond to the banjo by calling *take it*. Take it means that the guard will block the man on him and that the tackle will block the second backside lineman.

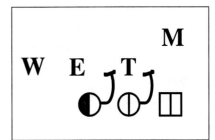

Figure 3-13. Take it

Backside tackle's rule (Figures 3-14 and 3-15): When the backside tackle is unaffected by a call, he'll block the first backside lineman (Figure 3-14). If he's on the openside versus a 30 stack look, he'll zone the stack to the linebacker (Figure 3-15).

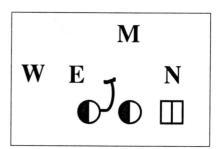

Figure 3-14. Backside tackle's rule

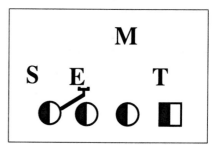

Figure 3-15. Backside tackle vs. 30 stack

Backside tight end's rule (Figure 3-16): The backside tight end will block the third backside defender.

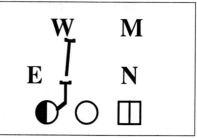

Figure 3-16. Backside tight end's rule

Tango (Figure 3-17): If a backside tight end exists, the backside tackle will call *tango* versus a 30 stack look, which means that he and the tight end will scoop combo the 4 or 5 technique to the backside backer.

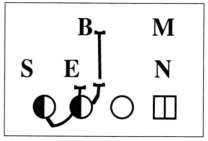

Figure 3-17. Tango

Although the number of calls that must be made may seem intimidating, remember that the only person who has to know them all is the offensive line coach. When coaching the zone scheme, coaching the mental aspects is just as important as coaching the physical aspects. A player who knows his assignment is a confident player, and a confident player can, to some extent, make up for a lack of physical talent.

In order to teach assignments, coaching the huddle is essential. Players don't have to process all at once all the information they get in the huddle. Three aspects of the game players should concentrate on in the huddle are: what's the scheme, am I playside or backside, and the snap count.

Once he leaves the huddle, a playside guard knows he only has to determine if he's covered (cage) or uncovered (tag) when he gets to the line of scrimmage. If no tag has been called, the playside tackle needs to know if he's covered or uncovered (Ted or Tex). The playside tight end only needs to respond to the tackle's call (Ted or Tex) or block the man on him.

The center knows he has to respond to a guard's call (cage or smash) or else he'll call Eagle if he and the playside guard are covered. The backside guard knows that he'll call uno, smash, or banjo depending on the alignment of the defensive tackle. The backside tackle knows he'll block the first backside lineman unless he gets a call from the guard (banjo). The backside tight end knows he'll block the third backside defender.

Once players get to the line, their calls are all based on their perceptions. They're coached as to what covered and uncovered look like, but in the end, what they think they see is what matters. The team will execute what gets called and live with it. If a player knows why he called what he did, it means they understand the scheme.

It's true that unusual circumstances demand special calls, such as fire, wide, Zorro, Eagle, take it, or tango. But none of these are crucial to the basic scheme. All of these can be introduced to them and then referred to again when they're needed versus specific opponents.

4

Wide Zone Blocking Techniques

The wide zone, rather than the tight zone, is the base play in the run game. The keys to the play are the techniques of the offensive linemen and the tailback's read. The appeal of the play is that it's a simple and physical concept that takes what the defense will give. It could be argued that it's the only run play needed in the run game because it threatens the whole defensive front and can be run from many different formations.

The technique used by a covered playside lineman is called *stretch base*:

- If a lineman is covered, he'll use enough of a lateral reach step to place his playside foot at a 45-degree angle outside the outside foot of the defensive lineman. The first step should emphasize width rather than gaining ground. If the defensive lineman is playing an extremely wide technique, it may be necessary to lose ground on the first step.

- The second step is the power step; the inside foot and knee should be brought to the crotch of the defensive lineman, with vertical movement being the point of emphasis. The inside hand should punch the sternum and the outside arm should press the outside pad.

- Without a call, the covered man has the defensive lineman by himself. The blocker should maintain flat pads as he works for position, but if he feels the man trying to come back inside, he should be heavy with the inside hand and work for inside/out position with his feet. Versus an inside slant, the blocker must sink with the defensive lineman until he's physically delivered into the block of an adjacent lineman.

- With a call, the covered man doesn't worry about the slant but will stay on course for the scraping linebacker. Without a slant, he executes the block, preparing to come off on the backer if the defender hangs on his back pad and the backer moves to the outside.

The technique used by the uncovered playside lineman is called *stretch double*:

- The uncovered man will open his hips and target the face mask of the defensive lineman. On the first step, he reads the near foot and knee of the defender. An inside slant will be taken over by the uncovered man. If the man doesn't slant, the uncovered man attacks the defender with both hands. If the defender hangs on the covered man's back pad, the uncovered man should shove him into the covered man's reach block. If the defender moves to the outside and the uncovered man doesn't make contact on his third step, he should get vertical to the second level for the backer.
- The coach must keep it as simple as possible as to which lineman will come off the combo to the backer. The covered man will come off on the backer if the defensive lineman slants inside or if the defender hangs on his back pad and the backer moves to the outside. He should stay on the lineman as long as possible and not worry about the backer until he shows up. If the defensive lineman plays across his face, then he never comes off on the backer.
- The uncovered man will come off on the backer if he doesn't make contact with the defensive lineman on his third step. If the lineman hangs on the back pad of the covered man, the uncovered man should continue to shove him outside until the backer does something. If the backer flows outside, the uncovered man should stay on the lineman. If the backer fills or squats inside, the uncovered man should come off on the backer. He should never allow the backer to hang back so he has to come under the combo.
- Versus a stacked backer, a team should simply execute stretch base and stretch double until the backer does something. If he moves outside, the covered man takes him, and if he stays or moves inside, the uncovered man takes him.

While all this sounds complicated, a coach can teach it if it's drilled correctly. Repetition is the key and is the reason that too many blocking schemes should be avoided if a coach chooses this blocking technique. The objective of the drill is to eliminate all thinking on the part of the offensive linemen and to simply allow them to react.

The drill is a two-on-two drill: two offensive linemen versus a defensive lineman and a linebacker. In other words, one offensive man will be covered and one uncovered. The drill is set up to allow the offensive players to be successful. The defensive lineman is instructed to use just enough force to make the offensive men work at establishing movement but to allow them to "win."

The defenders will use handheld dummies or arm shields or will simply be "human dummies." The defensive lineman will be aligned head-up or in an outside shade on one of the offensive linemen. The linebacker will be aligned over the uncovered lineman. The coach will stand behind the two offensive linemen and give signals to the defenders before calling the snap count. The first signal is for the defensive lineman and the second is for the linebacker.

The coach must keep it simple and not overcoach the drill. A defensive lineman can really do only three things and the backer's movements depend on what the down lineman does:

- The signal given to the defensive players is a fist in the air, which means the defensive lineman gets reached by the offensive lineman but maintains contact with the blocker and plays on his back pad. In this case, the backer has the option of playing behind the combo or flowing over the top. If the coach points at the backer, he's telling the backer to fill.
- Pointing to the outside tells the defensive lineman to move to the outside, thus playing across the face of the offensive lineman and preventing a reach block. In this case, the backer will flow behind the combo. Pointing at the backer means fill behind the combo.
- Pointing to the inside tells the defensive lineman to slant to the inside, which means the backer will flow over the top of the combo. Crossing the arms tells the backer to fill off the outside hip of the slanter.

With the blockers operating in pairs, alternating between covered and uncovered, and with the coach controlling the defensive players, offensive linemen can be quickly exposed to all possible situations. Each pair gets one repetition before they become the defensive players who service the next pair in line. Figure 4-1 illustrates the combo drill.

Figure 4-1. Combo drill

An essential variation of the drill is to place the defensive lineman in an inside shade on the covered man, with the backer shading outside the defensive lineman. When confronted with an inside shade, the covered man should take just enough of a lateral step so his second step will be in the defender's crotch.

The stretch base blocker should use his inside flipper rather than his hands so his outside arm is free and so he won't get his shoulders turned. An inside shade indicates that he's responsible for that gap and that the backer is responsible for the outside gap. Therefore, the stretch base should come off the combo as soon as he feels the stretch double blocker "on" the defender (Figure 4-2). The stretch double blocker will anticipate taking over the defensive lineman versus an inside shade; his aiming point will widen to the defender's playside number.

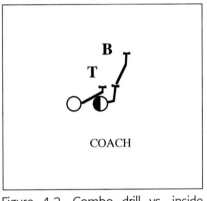

Figure 4-2. Combo drill vs. inside shade

The second element of the play is the read of the tailback. The tailback aims for the rear end of the tight end and reads the man on the tackle or the first man outside if the tackle is uncovered. As he presses the aiming point, he makes a decision to either stay outside the block on the key or to go inside. If he stays outside, he stays on course until something forces him to make a vertical cut. If he decides to run inside the key, he makes a vertical cut and "feels" his secondary read, which would be the guard or center's block on the defensive tackle. In many cases, the back will end up running inside the stretch block on the defensive tackle.

The back must understand that he must live with his decision and that it's a one-cut play, with no dancing in the hole. It's a team concept designed to keep the offense on schedule, with the worst-case scenario being no gain.

Again, repetition is paramount. The best way to drill the back's read is a team half line drill (Figures 4-3 and 4-4). The drill can be half speed or full speed and executed with the same mentality as the two-on-two offensive line drills. In other words, the offense "wins" with no tackle on the back. The signals by the offensive line coach remain the same but this time applies to the entire defense.

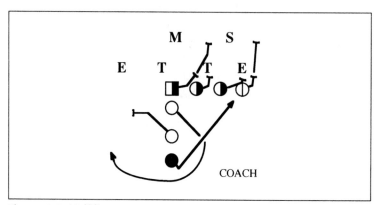

Figure 4-3. Half line vs. 43 over

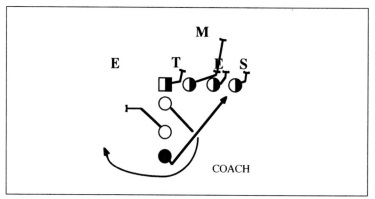

Figure 4-4. Half line vs. 43 under

The third element of the play is the backside. The backside blocking is actually more important than the playside because other than a bad read by the tailback, a loss on the play is most likely to result from a failure to control the backside pursuit. Note that the center may be considered backside or playside depending on whether he's covered. If he's uncovered, he's playside, and if he's covered, he's backside.

Backside combos use a scoop technique, with both blockers aiming for the playside armpit of the defensive lineman aligned on the inside blocker (Figure 4-5). The inside blocker is trying to escape to the backside backer but will stay on the defensive lineman as long as possible, with the flow of the backer determining when the inside man should come off the combo. The outside blocker will turn his hips and lose ground on

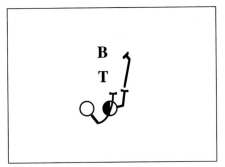

Figure 4-5. Scoop combo

his first step so he can overtake the defensive lineman's playside armpit. The scoop combo is drilled by using the same two-on-two drill used for the playside combos.

When a backside man isn't involved in a scoop combo, he'll use a wide reach block to block the defender who's on him. When a backside blocker must block a defender by himself who's one man removed, he'll use a scramble reach block. Examples would be a backside guard blocking a backside 1 technique, a backside tackle blocking a backside 3 technique, and a backside tight end blocking a backside 5 technique.

The scramble reach block is initiated by a flat step parallel to the line of scrimmage and then chasing the playside leg of the defender. The block shouldn't be executed until the blocker is able to deliver a blow with his backside flipper to the playside leg of the target. The block should be as low as possible, with the blocker converting to hands and feet, after driving the backside arm past the playside leg of the defender. The blocker should then attempt to get vertical, with his face to the goal line as he finishes the block by crab-walking on hands and feet. If the blocker starts to lose contact with the defender, the blocker should roll back into the man's legs. Backside individual blocks must be worked on at least once a week in season.

In season, combo drills should be specific to positions and the defensive looks anticipated from the next opponent. The offensive line coach can drill centers and guards on cage and smash combos, while the tight end coach drills tackles and tight ends on Ted and tango combos.

The tight ends and centers can then be dismissed to join quarterbacks and/or wide receivers while the offensive line coach drills guards and tackles on tag and banjo combos. After the combo drills are completed, the centers can return and the interior line can work on pass protections.

Wide Zone

Figure 5-1 illustrates wide zone versus 43 over. The playside guard calls *cage* because he's covered. He and the center combo the 3 technique to the Mike backer. The playside tackle calls *Ted* because he's uncovered. He and the tight end combo the 6 technique to the second backer, counting from Mike. The backside guard calls *uno* and blocks the backside 1 technique. The backside tackle blocks the backside backer. The fullback blocks the backside C gap.

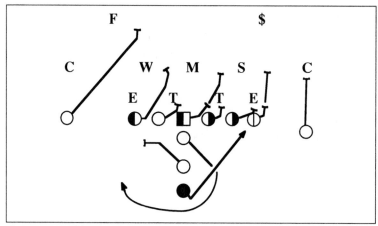

Figure 5-1. Wide zone vs. 43 over

Figure 5-2 illustrates wide zone versus 43 under. The playside guard calls *tag* because he's uncovered. He and the tackle combo the 5 technique to the first playside backer. The center blocks the playside 1 technique and the tight end blocks the 9 technique. The backside guard calls *banjo* because he's covered and there is no 0 technique; he and the backside tackle scoop combo the 3 technique to the backside backer. The fullback blocks the backside C gap.

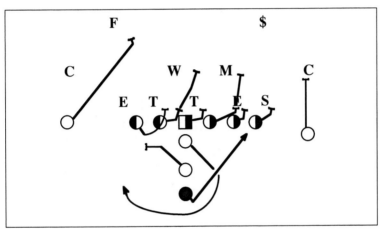

Figure 5-2. Wide zone vs. 43 under

Figure 5-3 illustrates wide zone versus a 44 defense. The playside guard calls *cage* because he's covered. He and the center combo the 3 technique to the first playside backer. The tackle calls *Ted* because he's uncovered. He and the tight end combo the 6 technique to the second playside backer. The backside guard calls *uno* and blocks the backside 1 technique. The backside tackle blocks the backside backer. The fullback blocks the backside C gap.

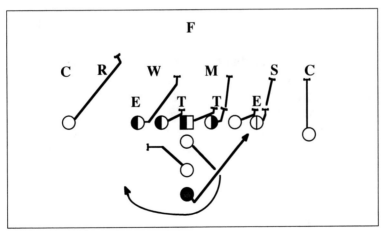

Figure 5-3. Wide zone vs. 44

Figure 5-4 illustrates wide zone versus 30 stack. The playside guard calls *tag* because he's uncovered. He and the tackle combo the 5 technique to the first playside backer. The tight end blocks the 9 technique. The backside guard calls *smash* because a 0 technique is being played on the center. He and the center scoop combo the 0 technique to the Mike backer. The backside tackle zones the stack and the fullback blocks the backside C gap.

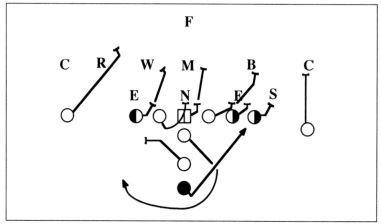

Figure 5-4. Wide zone vs. 30 stack

By attaching words to the play call, offensive players can solve problems that some defenses may present. In most cases, these words enable playside combos to go to the backside backer if the playside backer doesn't fill. In effect, this creates two combos to the backside backer.

Wide Zone Force

The word *force* tells the fullback to block a contain defender who's aligned in the short zone outside the tight end. Figure 5-5 illustrates wide zone force versus a 44 defense. The playside tackle calls *Tex* instead of *Ted* when he's uncovered with a force huddle call. He and the tight end will combo the 6 technique to the first backer in the box. The fullback will block the force player. The guard calls *cage* because he's covered. He and the center will combo the 3 technique to the Mike or to the backside backer if no Mike exists. They know they can go to the backside backer when they hear the tackle's Tex call. The backside guard calls *uno* and blocks the backside 1 technique. The backside tackle blocks the backside backer.

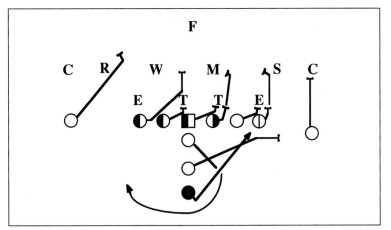

Figure 5-5. Wide zone force vs. 44

If no force player exists, as would be encountered versus a four deep secondary (Figure 5-6), the fullback will aim for the rear end of the playside tackle, reading the same run key that the tailback reads. The fullback will block the most dangerous defender—either inside or outside the tackle's block depending on what the run key does.

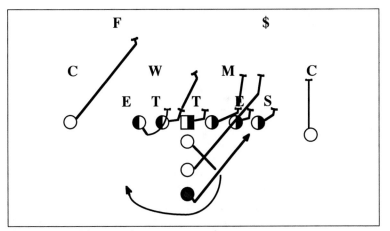

Figure 5-6. Wide zone force vs. 43 under

Wide Zone Blast

Another word that can be added to the play call is the word *blast*. Blast is a way to solve the problem of a playside backer who's difficult to block, which is most prevalent when the backer is stacked behind a defensive lineman. Like the force call, blast also enables two combos to the backside backer if no Mike backer exists. In blast, the fullback is assigned to block the first playside backer.

Figure 5-7 illustrates wide zone blast versus 43 under. Against a playside 1 technique, the guard will call *ace*, which means that he and the center will combo the 1 technique to the backside backer. The playside tackle and tight end block the 5 and 9 techniques, respectively. The fullback aims for the tackle's rear end and blocks through or around to the playside backer. The backside guard calls *banjo* and he and the backside tackle scoop combo the 3 technique to the backside backer.

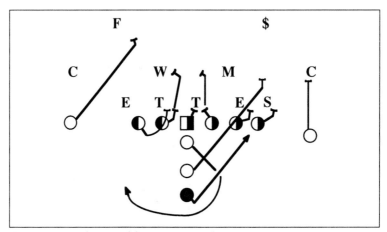

Figure 5-7. Wide zone blast vs. 43 under

Figure 5-8 illustrates wide zone blast versus a 44 defense. The playside guard calls *cage* because he's covered. He and the center combo the 3 technique to the backside backer because they know that the word *blast* puts the fullback on the playside backer. The fullback aims for the tackle's rear end and blocks through or around to the playside backer. The tackle calls *Ted* because he's uncovered. He and the tight end combo the 6 technique to the second playside backer. The backside guard calls *uno* and blocks the backside 1 technique. The backside tackle blocks the backside backer.

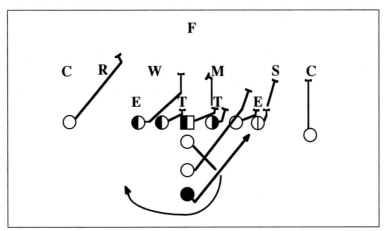

Figure 5-8. Wide zone blast vs. 44

When wide zone is run to the split end side from a two-back formation, the fullback must be a lead blocker. His assignment is to block the force defender or to aim for the tackle's rear end and block the most dangerous defender if no force player exists.

Wide Zone Bob

- The preferred way to run wide zone to the split end side is to attach the word *Bob* to the play call.
- The fullback blocks the force defender or the first playside backer if no force defender exists.
- As in blast, the cage combo will work backside because it's assumed that the fullback is blocking the playside backer. Also, as in blast, the playside guard calls ace versus a playside 1 technique, which means that he and the center will combo the 1 technique to the Mike or backside backer.
- It's the tackle's responsibility to call *base* to the guard and center if a force defender exists. Base means the fullback will be blocking force rather than the playside backer. Therefore, playside combos will work to the playside backer rather than the backside backer.

Figure 5-9 illustrates wide zone Bob versus 43 under. The playside tackle blocks the 5 technique. The fullback aims for the tackle's rear end and blocks through or around to the playside backer. The playside guard calls *cage* because he's covered; he and the center combo the 3 technique to the backside backer. The backside guard calls *uno* and blocks the backside 1 technique. The backside tackle blocks the backside backer. The backside tight end blocks the 5 technique because he's the third backside defender.

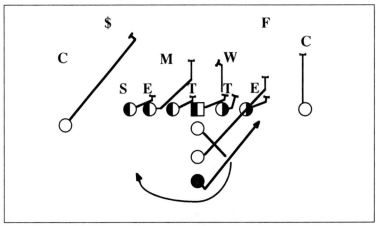

Figure 5-9. Wide zone Bob vs. 43 under

Figure 5-10 illustrates wide zone Bob versus 43 over. The playside tackle blocks the 5 technique. The fullback aims for the tackle's rear end and blocks through or around to the playside backer. The playside guard calls *ace* versus a playside 1 technique; he and the center combo the 1 technique to the Mike backer. The backside guard calls

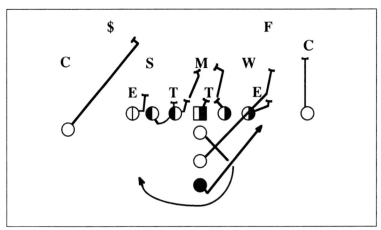

Figure 5-10. Wide zone Bob vs. 43 over

banjo because no 0 or backside 1 technique is being played and he's covered. He and the backside tackle execute a scoop combo on the 3 technique to the backside backer. The backside tight end blocks the 6 technique because he's the third backside defender.

When wide zone Bob is run versus eight-man fronts, the tackle must call *base* because the fullback must now block the force defender. Therefore, it's best to run the play to twin receivers because the defense is now forced to play the force defender on the slot receiver. Figure 5-11 illustrates twins, wide zone Bob versus a 44 defense. The playside tackle blocks the 5 technique. The fullback aims for the tackle's rear end and blocks through or around to the playside backer. The playside guard calls *ace* because a playside 1 technique is being played; he and the center combo the 1 technique to the backside backer. The backside guard calls *banjo* because no 0 or backside 1 technique is being played and he's covered. He and the backside tackle execute a scoop combo on the 3 technique to the backside backer. The backside tight end blocks the 6 technique because he's the third backside defender.

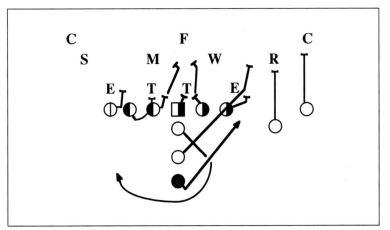

Figure 5-11. Twins, wide zone Bob vs. 44

One-Back Wide Zone

Wide zone can be run to a tight end from any one-back formation. One-back formations can give a blocking advantage against some defensive looks. As an example, a 43 under that wishes to remain in cover 2 has an adjustment problem versus a two-tight-end-and-one-back formation and must adjust the front to the wideside of the field. To the boundary side, the defensive end must play a 6 or 7 technique and the defense is outnumbered to that side.

Figure 5-12 illustrates the advantage that the offense enjoys when it runs wide zone into the boundary. The playside tackle will call *Tex* instead of *Ted* because no second playside backer exists. He and the tight end will combo to the first backer in the box. When the playside guard and center hear *Tex*, they know that the guard's cage call can now combo to the backside backer. The backside guard calls *uno* and blocks the backside 1 technique. The backside tackle blocks the backside backer. The backside tight end blocks the 5 technique because he's the third backside defender.

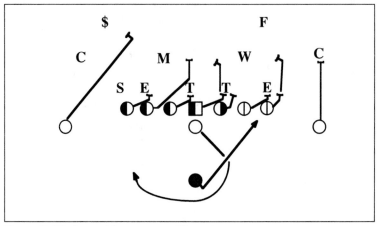

Figure 5-12. Ace, wide zone vs. 43 under

The trips formation forces defenses playing zone coverage to adjust by aligning a linebacker on the slot receiver. The scheme advantage that has been gained is illustrated by Figure 5-13. The adjustment made by a 44 defense enables the playside tackle to call *Tex* instead of *Ted* because the second playside backer has been removed by the defensive adjustment. In turn, the Tex call allows the cage combo to work to the

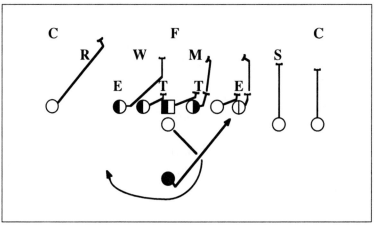

Figure 5-13. Trips, wide zone vs. 44

backside backer. The backside guard calls *uno* and blocks the backside 1 technique. The backside tackle blocks the backside backer.

When wide zone is run to the split end side of a one-back formation, the team should use a "check with me" call in the huddle. The play call is to the split end side, with a second play to the tight end side also called. The rule to use for the quarterback is the rule of two; if he sees two backers, counting from a Mike backer to the force area, the play must be checked to the tight end side. Any force player is considered a backer, whether he's on or off the line of scrimmage. Figure 5-14 illustrates a defensive alignment against which the play should be checked to the tight end side because the Mike backer counts as one backer and the Will backer counts as the second.

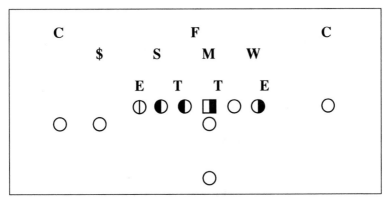

Figure 5-14. Rule of two; the play must be checked.

Figure 5-15 illustrates a solution to the problem by the deployment of a slot receiver to that side, which forces the second backer (Will) to align in coverage. Against this look, the play would be run and not checked to the tight end side because the slot can block the second backer. If a coach is reluctant to allow his quarterback to check plays,

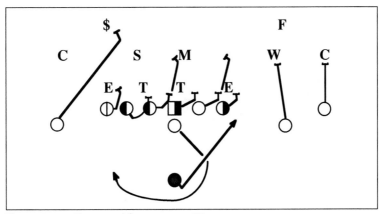

Figure 5-15. Space, wide zone vs. 43 over

the play shouldn't be called to the split end side from a one-back formation unless the players have absolute assurance that the defensive adjustment won't have more than one backer to that side.

Wide Zone Reverse

When the backside defensive end begins to chase wide zone, the wide zone reverse (Figure 5-16) should be run.

- All linemen block wide zone away from the point of attack.
- The playside guard and tackle will execute backside techniques for two counts and will then release as lead blockers.
- The fullback will give the appearance of cutting off the defensive end as he does on wide zone and will then pin him to the inside.

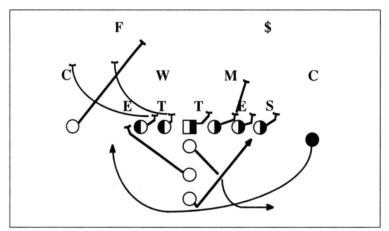

Figure 5-16. Wide zone reverse

6

Tight Zone

The tight zone system uses the wide zone as the base and adapts the tight zone techniques to it. Tight zone is a complement to the wide zone and is blocked with the same techniques and line calls, with minor adjustments to the technique of the uncovered man. The approach taken should be to establish the wide zone play and to run the tight zone after the defense is flowing hard to stop that play. For that reason most practice time is devoted to wide zone, with tight zone receiving about one third of the time devoted to wide zone. In the minds of the players, the thought process of tight zone should be as similar as possible to wide zone.

- In the interest of simplicity, this system makes no difference at all to a playside covered lineman between wide zone and tight zone.
- *Tight base* is identical to stretch base; the covered man will stay on the combo as long as possible, and assuming that the defender hasn't crossed his face, the covered man will come off on the backer only if he shows up.
- The playside adjustment is to the uncovered man's technique.
- *Tight double* changes the aiming point to the near hip of the defensive lineman rather than the face mask, as in stretch double.
- The uncovered man will take a reach step but will square his shoulders on the second step, pressing the defensive lineman with his playside hand.
- The uncovered man will stay on the double-team as long as possible and will come off the combo to the backer if he fills or remains behind the combo.

- If the uncovered man doesn't achieve contact on the defensive lineman on his second step, he works to the second level.
- Because a high probability of a cutback exists, a coach should also change backside techniques.
- If a backside lineman must block a man who's one man removed by himself, he won't scramble block but will use a *ram* block. The technique of the ram block is to step flat and get your head in front and then push the man into the pile if the lineman is unable to reach him. The key factor is to prevent penetration and let the back find the cutback lane.
- Practicing the techniques for tight zone uses the same two-on-two drills as the wide zone. All calls are identical to wide zone. The back's read is practiced by using the same team half line drill.
- The tailback will now square his shoulders on the third step and aim for the inside leg of the tackle. The tailback's read is now the block on the first defensive lineman outside the A gap. The tailback must press the line of scrimmage and make his cut at the heels of the offensive linemen.

Figure 6-1 illustrates tight zone versus 43 over. The playside guard calls *cage* because he's covered. He and the center combo the 3 technique to the Mike backer. The playside tackle calls *Ted* because he's uncovered. He and the tight end combo the 6 technique to the Sam backer, because he's the second backer, counting from the Mike backer. The backside guard calls *uno* and blocks the backside 1 technique. The backside tackle blocks the backside backer. The fullback blocks the backside C gap.

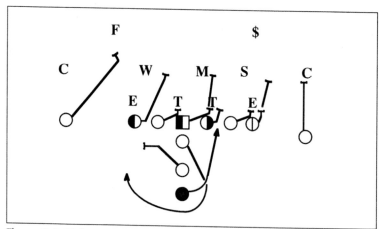

Figure 6-1. Tight zone vs. 43 over

Figure 6-2 illustrates tight zone versus 43 under. The playside guard calls *tag* because he's uncovered. He and the tackle combo the 5 technique to the first playside backer. The center blocks the playside 1 technique and the tight end blocks the 9 technique. The backside guard calls *banjo* because he's covered and there is no 0 technique; he and the backside tackle scoop combo the 3 technique to the backside backer. The fullback blocks the backside C gap.

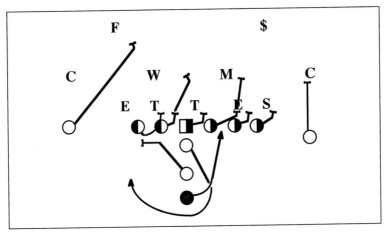

Figure 6-2. Tight zone vs. 43 under

When the play is run against an eight-man front and the unblocked backside force player becomes a problem, it's best to run the play from twins formation because he can now be blocked by the slot receiver. Figure 6-3 illustrates twins, tight zone versus 44. The playside guard calls *cage* because he's covered. He and the center combo

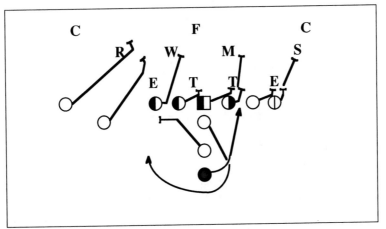

Figure 6-3. Twins, tight zone vs. 44

the 3 technique to the playside backer. The playside tackle calls *Ted* because he's uncovered. He and the tight end combo the 6 technique to the second playside. The backside guard calls *uno* and blocks the backside 1 technique. The backside tackle blocks the backside backer. The fullback blocks the backside C gap.

Unlike wide zone, the term *force* isn't applied to tight zone. However, the term *blast* is applied with the caveat that someone must account for the backside C gap. This is true because of the high probability that the play will cut back to the backside. Either the play should be run from a two-tight-end formation or a wide receiver should motion to a position where he can block the backside C gap.

Figure 6-4 illustrates tight zone blast from a two-tight-end formation. Against a playside 1 technique, the guard will call *ace*, which means that he and the center will combo the 1 technique to the backside backer. The playside tackle and tight end block the 5 and 9 techniques, respectively. The fullback blocks the playside backer. The backside guard calls *banjo* and he and the backside tackle scoop combo the 3 technique to the backside backer.

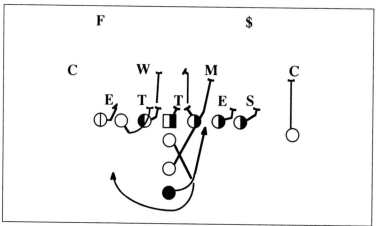

Figure 6-4. Tight zone blast vs. 43 under

Tight Zone Bob

When the play is run to the split end side from a two-back formation, the term *Bob* is applied as in wide zone. As in wide zone Bob, the fullback blocks the force player or first playside backer if there is no force player. Also, as in wide zone Bob, the *cage* call works to the backside backer and the playside guard calls *ace* versus a playside 1 technique. Figure 6-5 illustrates tight zone Bob versus 43 over. The playside tackle blocks the 5 technique. The fullback blocks the first playside backer. The playside guard calls *ace* versus a playside 1 technique; he and the center combo the 1 technique to the Mike backer. The backside guard calls *banjo* because he's covered and there is no 0 technique; he and the backside tackle scoop combo the 3 technique to the backside backer. The backside tight end blocks the 6 technique because he's the third backside defender.

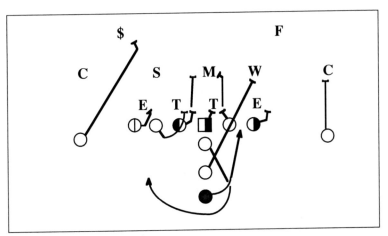

Figure 6-5. Tight zone Bob vs. 43 over

Versus an eight-man front, running the play to twins formation is best because the force defender must now align on the slot receiver. Figure 6-6 illustrates tight zone Bob versus a 44 defense. The playside tackle blocks the 5 technique. The fullback blocks the first playside backer. The playside guard calls *ace* because there is a playside 1 technique; he and the center combo the 1 technique to the backside backer. The backside guard calls *banjo* because he's covered and there is no 0 technique; he and the backside tackle scoop combo the 3 technique to the backside backer. The backside tight end blocks the 6 technique because he's the third backside defender.

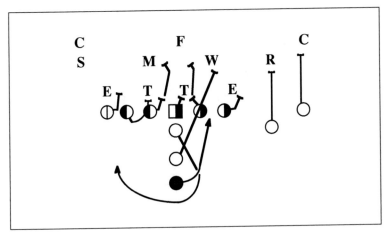

Figure 6-6. Twins, tight zone Bob vs. 44

One-Back Tight Zone

When the play is run from a one-back formation, the same problem of accounting for the backside C gap exists as in blast, and the same solutions may be applied. Figure 6-7 illustrates one-back tight zone from a two-tight-end formation versus 30 stack. The playside guard calls *tag* because he's uncovered. He and the tackle combo the 5 technique to the first playside backer. The tight end blocks the 9 technique. The backside guard calls *smash* because a 0 technique is being played on the center. He and the center scoop combo the 0 technique to the Mike backer. The backside tackle calls *tango* versus 30 stack; he and the tight end combo the 5 technique to the backside backer.

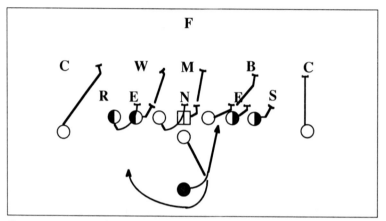

Figure 6-7. Ace, tight zone vs. 30 stack

When the play is run from a one-back formation to the split end side (Figure 6-8), the same "rule of two" check as in wide zone should be used by the quarterback

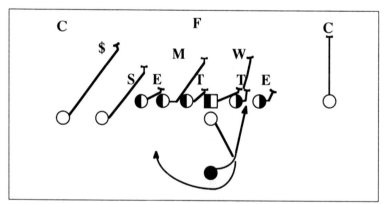

Figure 6-8. Trips, tight zone vs. 43 under

when more than one linebacker is to that side. However, the play checked to should be wide zone strong instead of tight zone strong because of the problem of the unblocked backside C gap. Figure 6-9 illustrates tight zone against a defense that has only one linebacker to the split end side. Once again, if a coach is reluctant to allow his quarterback to check plays, the play shouldn't be called to the split end side from a one-back formation unless the coach is sure that the defensive adjustment will have only one linebacker to that side.

Tight Zone Counter

When the backside C gap defender becomes difficult for the fullback to block, the tight zone counter should be used. All linemen block tight zone and the fullback pins the C gap defender inside. Figure 6-9 illustrates tight zone counter.

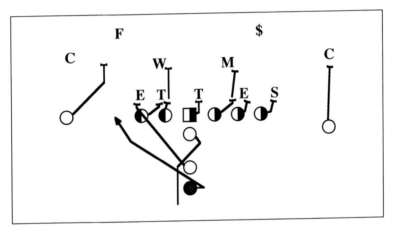

Figure 6-9. Tight zone counter

Fullback Dive

The fullback dive (Figure 6-10) is also a tight zone play. It's run to the tight end side only. A fake pitch after the handoff controls the backside defensive end. If the defensive end doesn't respect the fake pitch, the pitch play should be called. As in tight zone counter, all linemen simply block the play as a tight zone (Figure 6-11).

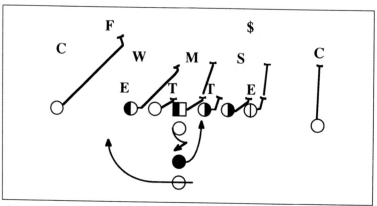

Figure 6-10. Fullback dive

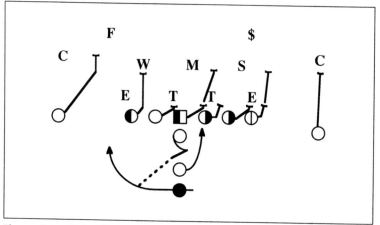

Figure 6-11. Fake dive pitch

7

The Option

The option is a wide zone play with adjustments. When option is part of the huddle call, the playside tackle will call *Tex* instead of *Ted* when he's uncovered. Tex means that the tackle and tight end will combo the man on the tight end to the first backer in the box, rather than the second playside backer. The Tex call also allows the cage combo of the playside guard and center to work to the Mike or backside backer rather than to the playside backer. The quarterback will then option the first defender outside the box (Figure 7-1).

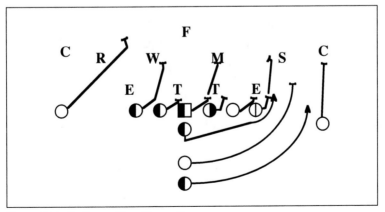

Figure 7-1. Option with a Tex call

Option Seal

When the term *seal* is attached to the play call, the tight end will call *seal* when he's covered by a 9 technique. Seal means that the tight end will block the first backer in the box, counting from outside in, and that the quarterback will now option the 9 technique. The seal technique is to step with the outside foot and help the tackle block the 5 technique with the inside hand as the second step is taken (Figure 7-2). If no 9 technique is being played, the tight end will block normal zone rule.

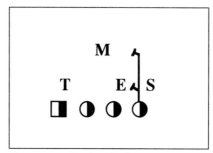

Figure 7-2. Seal technique

Figure 7-3 illustrates option seal versus 43 under. The tight end calls *seal* because he's covered by a 9 technique; he then releases inside the 9 technique and blocks the first backer in the box. The playside guard calls *tag* because he's uncovered. The seal call by the tight end enables the tag combo to work to the backside backer if the playside backer doesn't fill. The center blocks the playside 1 technique. The backside guard calls *banjo* because he's covered and there is no 0 technique; he and the backside tackle scoop combo the 3 technique to the backside backer.

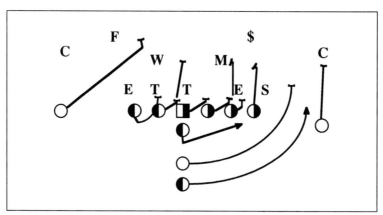

Figure 7-3. Option seal vs. 43 under

When the playside tackle is uncovered with a seal call, he'll use the same seal technique as the tight end by helping the guard block the 3 technique with his inside hand as he moves to block the second backer in the box. Figure 7-4 illustrates option seal versus 43 over wide. The tight end calls *seal* because he's covered by a 9 technique; he then releases inside the 9 technique and blocks the first backer in the box. The playside tackle seals the second backer in the box because he's uncovered. The playside guard calls *cage* because he's covered. He and the center combo the 3 technique to the Mike backer. The backside guard calls *uno* and blocks the backside 1 technique. The backside tackle blocks the backside backer.

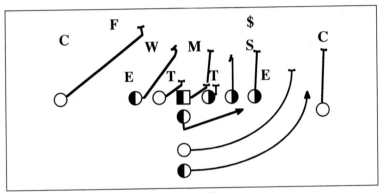

Figure 7-4. Option seal vs. 43 over wide

When option is run to the split end side, the term *seal* may also be applied. The term *seal* on the split end side tells the playside tackle to not block the defensive end. The defensive end is defined as the last defender who's on the line of scrimmage, regardless of whether he's a backer or defensive back. If he's on the line, he's the defensive end. If the tackle is covered by the defensive end, he'll call *seal* and then block the first backer in the box, counting from outside in by using the same seal technique as the tight end does on option seal.

Figure 7-5 illustrates option seal versus 43 under. The playside tackle calls *seal* because he's covered by the defensive end; he then releases inside the defensive

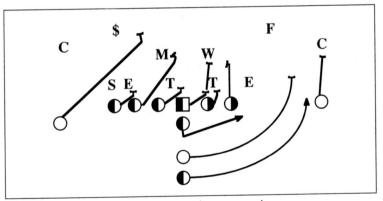

Figure 7-5. Split end side option seal vs. 43 under

end and blocks the first backer in the box. The playside guard calls *cage* because he's covered; he and the center combo the 3 technique to the backside backer. The backside guard calls *uno* and blocks the 1 technique. The backside tackle blocks the backside backer and the backside tight end blocks the 5 technique because he's the third backside defender.

When the playside guard is uncovered and receives a seal call from the tackle, he'll use the same seal technique as the tackle to block the second backer in the box. Figure 7-6 illustrates option seal versus 43 over. The playside tackle calls *seal* because he's covered by the defensive end; he then releases inside the defensive end and blocks the first backer in the box. The playside guard seals the second backer in the box because he's uncovered. The center blocks the 1 technique. The backside guard calls *banjo* because he's covered and there is no 0 technique; he and the backside tackle scoop combo the 3 technique to the backside backer. The backside tight end blocks the 6 technique because he's the third backside defender.

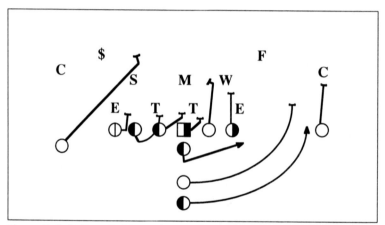

Figure 7-6. Split end side option seal vs. 43 over

When the playside tackle isn't covered by the defensive end, he won't call seal and will block normal zone rule. Figure 7-7 illustrates option seal versus a 34 defense in which the Will backer is aligned on the line of scrimmage, thus making him the defensive end. The playside guard calls *tag* because he's uncovered; he and the tackle combo the 5 technique to the playside backer. The backside guard calls *smash* because a 0 technique is being played on the center; he and the center combo the 0 technique to the backside backer. The backside tackle blocks the 5 technique because he's the first backside lineman and the backside tight end blocks the 9 technique because he's the third backside defender.

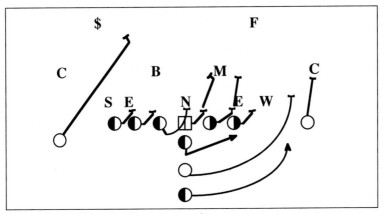

Figure 7-7. Split end side option seal vs. 34

The term *seal crack* tells the split end or the slot in twins to crack the first unblocked backer inside. The playside tackle can now work to the second backer if the first backer flows. Figure 7-8 illustrates option seal crack versus a 44 defense. The playside tackle calls *seal* because he's covered by the defensive end; he then releases inside the defensive end and blocks the first backer he has leverage on. The playside guard seals the second backer in the box because he's uncovered. The center blocks the 1 technique. The backside guard calls *banjo* because he's covered and there is no 0 technique; he and the backside tackle scoop combo the 3 technique to the backside backer. The backside tight end blocks the 6 technique because he's the third backside defender.

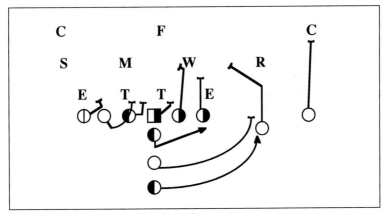

Figure 7-8. Twins, option seal crack vs. 44

One-Back Option

As in wide zone, option seal may find a numbers advantage when it's run from a two-tight-end-and-one-back formation. As an example, versus 43 under, cover 2, the defense will be outnumbered to the boundary side of the formation. Figure 7-9 illustrates option seal into the boundary versus 43 under. The playside tackle calls *Tex* because he's uncovered; he and the tight end combo the 6 technique to the first backer in the box. The playside guard calls *cage* because he's covered; he and the center combo the 3 technique to the backside backer. The backside guard calls *uno* and blocks the backside 1 technique. The backside tackle blocks the backside backer and the backside tight end blocks the 5 technique because he's the third backside defender.

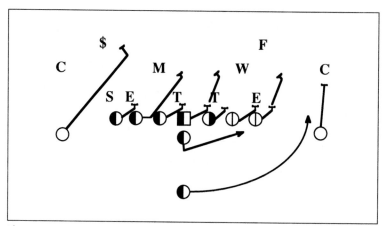

Figure 7-9. Ace, option seal vs. 43 under, cover 2

If the defense chooses to play cover 3 by bringing up the strong safety to the wideside while adjusting the front into the boundary, the offense gains a two-on-one advantage on the Sam backer when running option seal into the boundary. Figure 7-10 illustrates option seal into the boundary versus 43 under, cover 3. The playside tight end calls *seal* because he's covered by a 9 technique; he then releases inside the 9 technique and blocks the first backer in the box. The playside guard calls *tag* because he's uncovered; he and the tackle combo the 5 technique to the backside backer. The center blocks the playside 1 technique. The backside guard calls *banjo* because he's covered and there is no 0 technique; he and the backside tackle scoop combo the 3 technique to the backside backer. The backside tight end blocks the 6 technique because he's the third backside defender.

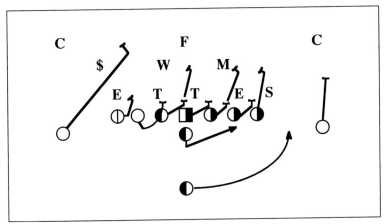

Figure 7-10. Ace, option seal vs. 43 under, cover 3

When the offense aligns in trips formation, a defense playing cover 2 must align a box linebacker on the slot, allowing the tight end and/or playside tackle to seal the box. The quarterback and pitchback essentially have a two-on-none advantage. Figure 7-11 illustrates trips, option seal versus 43 over. The playside tackle calls *Tex* because he's uncovered; he and the tight end combo the 6 technique to the first backer in the box. The playside guard calls *cage* because he's covered; he and the center combo the 3 technique to the backside backer. The backside guard calls *uno* and blocks the backside 1 technique. The backside tackle blocks the backside backer.

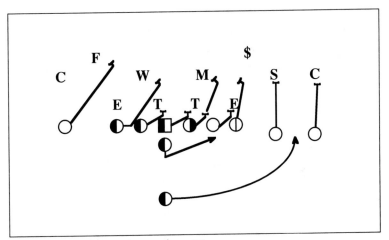

Figure 7-11. Trips, option seal vs. 43 over

When option seal is run from a one-back formation to the split end, the "check with me" rule of two should be applied. If two backers are to that side, the play should be checked strong. Running the play to twin receivers is preferred because one of the backers must align on the slot. Figure 7-12 illustrates space, option seal versus a 44 defense. The playside tackle calls *seal* because he's covered by the defensive end; he then releases inside the defensive end and blocks the first backer in the box. The playside guard seals the second backer in the box because he's uncovered. The center blocks the 1 technique. The backside guard calls *banjo* because he's covered and there is no 0 technique; he and the backside tackle scoop combo the 3 technique to the backside backer. The backside tight end blocks the 6 technique because he's the third backside defender.

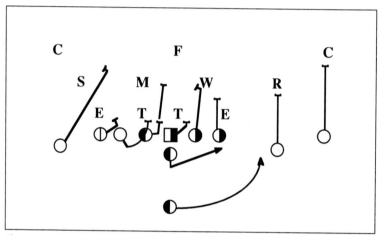

Figure 7-12. Space, option seal vs. 44

If the defensive end is playing tight on the playside tackle, the term *crack* simply says block wide zone with the split end or slot cracking on the playside backer. The quarterback will now option the next defender outside the defensive end (Figure 7-13).

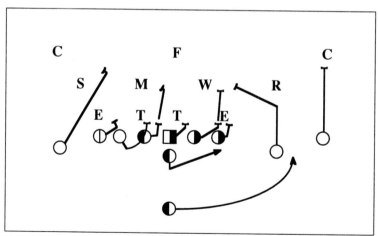

Figure 7-13. Space, option crack vs. 44

Option Reverse

As in wide zone, including a reverse in the option sequence can be useful. Linemen will execute the play as they do wide zone reverse, except the playside tackle will now peel back to block the C gap after blocking his backside zone technique for two counts. Figure 7-14 illustrates option reverse.

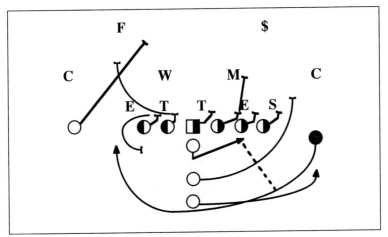

Figure 7-14. Option reverse

8

The Gap Scheme

Gap blocking is the complement to zone blocking. It may be thought of a reverse zone in that two linemen work in tandem versus a down lineman and linebacker, but they're working to their inside gap instead of their outside gap. The gap scheme has no calls. The rule and the priorities determine which linemen work together. Coaches can use gap scheme to make dummy zone calls to throw off the defenders who may have determined that certain zone calls mean playside or backside. When running gap scheme, the playside linemen will give backside zone calls and the backside linemen will give playside zone calls.

- All playside linemen have the same rule: Block the first inside lineman. An inside lineman is defined as an inside shade to head-up on the next offensive lineman inside.

- The technique used by an offensive lineman blocking a defensive lineman inside is called a *gap block*. The gap blocker will lose ground with his inside foot so his inside toe is pointed directly at the inside foot of the defender who's inside of him. His second step must get on the ground quickly as he aims his inside hand at the far pad and his face mask at the near number of the defender. The outside hand will punch the near pad.

- The point of emphasis is to deny penetration and to turn the hips and drive the defender to the inside after initial contact. If the defender plays soft and attempts to roll over the top, the lineman should control him with his hands and feet as he converts to a base block.

- The gap blocker should stay on course if the target slants to the inside. He should then proceed to the same backer that he would have blocked if no defensive linemen had been aligned inside of him.

If no inside defensive lineman exists, a playside lineman will block a linebacker. A playside tight end or playside tackle will block the second backer in the box, counting from outside in. The playside guard will block the first backside backer. However, a player should block any backer who fills his inside seam as he attempts to release to his assigned backer.

- The technique used by an offensive lineman who has no defensive lineman inside is to block the backside number of his assigned linebacker. A player should attack the backside number to prevent the backer from releasing under the block. He should think of the block on the backer as a gap block on a backer. If the backer attempts to roll over the top, he should convert to a base block on the backer, as he would a lineman who's rolling over the top.
- A playside lineman who's assigned to a linebacker will *post* the man on before releasing to the backer. The post technique doesn't apply to the tight end and won't apply to the tackle if no tight end is outside him.
- A lineman executing the post technique will take a small step inside with his inside foot so he can attack the inside number of the defender with his outside flipper as he steps straight upfield on his second step. The point of emphasis is to get the second step into the crotch of the defender and jack him up to help the gap blocker. Contact should be maintained for three to four steps before releasing for his assigned backer.
- If the defensive lineman slants to the inside, the post blocker should stay on him and the gap blocker will then stay on course to linebacker level.

The techniques of gap and post are practiced in much the same way that zone combos are practiced. In this case, the drill is two on three: one covered offensive lineman who's the post blocker and one offensive lineman outside of him who's the gap blocker. The drill has three defenders: a defensive lineman who aligns on the inside offensive lineman, a linebacker who aligns in the inside seam of the covered offensive lineman, and a second backer who aligns 2 to 3 yards inside the other backer.

The coach will stand behind the offensive linemen and give signals to the defenders. A fist in the air means that the defensive lineman will play base, with both backers flowing to their outside for two to three steps. If the coach points at the near backer, it means that the defensive lineman will play base, with the near backer filling the post blocker's inside seam and the far backer flowing over the top. If the coach points to the inside, it means that the defensive lineman will slant to his inside gap and that both backers will flow over the top. Figure 8-1 illustrates the gap drill.

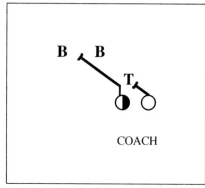

Figure 8-1. Gap drill

The assignments of the backside guard and fullback depend on whether the huddle call is power gap or counter gap.

- When power gap is the call, the backside guard will pull through the hole for the playside backer and the kick-out block will be performed by the fullback.
- The fullback will aim for the inside leg of the tackle and execute a kick-out block on the first defender to show outside the tackle's block.
- The guard will be hip-to-hip with the fullback and turn up inside his kick-out block. The guard should execute a kick-out block on the backer in the hole if possible. The guard must blow up any penetration between himself and the hole.

When counter gap is the call, the backside guard and fullback exchange assignments.

- The backside guard's assignment is to pull flat and execute a kick-out block on the first defender to show outside the playside tackle's block.
- The technique is *dip and rip*. As an example, a left guard pulling to the right would identify the target as he clears the center and explode with his right flipper into the inside number of the defender as he runs through the block. The blocker's head must be between the defender and the first down marker.
- The guard will adjust to the target's technique. If the defender is at the blocker's level, the guard will stay flat and execute dip and rip. If the defender is deeper than the blocker, the guard will stay flat until he's almost on target and then adjust to the defender's level. It's a mistake to get deep too quickly, as the defender could then fold back upfield of the guard's block. If the defender squats on the line of scrimmage, the guard will work up into the line and dig him out. If the defender moves inside so he can wrong-arm the blocker, the guard will seal his outside number.
- The fullback will run a two-step dive course to the backside and allow the quarterback to clear. He'll then redirect playside on his third step, on a course that will place him behind and 1 yard deeper than the pulling guard. The fullback will

turn up inside the guard's block and block the playside backer. The fullback will read the guard's block; if the guard seals a wrong-arm technique, the fullback will turn up outside the block and block the scraping backer. The ballcarrier can then bounce the play outside.

The center and backside tackle work together to seal off the backside A, B, and C gaps.

- If the backside guard is uncovered, the center will post the man on him before releasing to the backside backer.
- If the backside guard is covered, the center will block from A gap to B gap. The center steps at a 45-degree angle into the backside A gap and keys the backside backer for blitz; if a blitz occurs, the center blocks the A gap. If no blitz occurs, the center continues to the B gap and blocks the first backside lineman.
- The backside tackle's technique is called *bubble cutoff*; the tackle slide steps into the B gap and keys the backside backer for blitz. If a blitz occurs, the tackle stays in the B gap and blocks the B gap defender.
- If no blitz occurs, the tackle will pivot on his inside foot and block C gap pursuit when he's sure the center is blocking the B gap.

Power Gap

Figure 8-2 illustrates power gap versus 43 over. The playside tight end blocks the Mike backer because no lineman is inside of him and because the Mike backer is the second backer in the box. The playside tackle gap blocks the 3 technique. The playside guard posts the 3 technique and releases for the backside backer because no inside lineman exists. The center blocks the backside 1 technique. The backside guard pulls through the hole for the playside backer. The backside tackle executes a bubble cutoff. The fullback executes a kick-out block on the first defender to show outside the playside tackle.

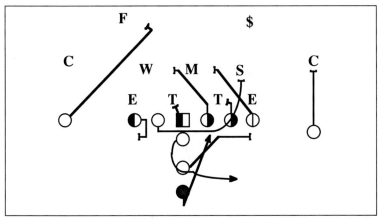

Figure 8-2. Power gap vs. 43 over

Figure 8-3 illustrates power gap versus 43 under. The playside tight end gap blocks the 5 technique. The playside tackle posts the 5 technique before releasing for the backside backer. The playside guard gap blocks the 1 technique. The center blocks back because the backside guard is covered. The backside guard pulls through the hole for the playside backer. The backside tackle executes a bubble cutoff. The fullback executes a kick-out block on the first defender to show outside the playside tackle.

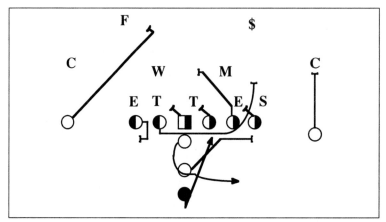

Figure 8-3. Power gap vs. 43 under

Figure 8-4 illustrates power gap versus a 44. When there is no inside lineman and only two backers are in the box, the tight end will arc release for the force player. The playside tackle gap blocks the 3 technique. The playside guard posts the 3 technique before releasing for the backside backer. The center blocks the backside 1 technique. The backside guard pulls through the hole for the playside backer. The backside tackle executes a bubble cutoff. The fullback executes a kick-out block on the first defender to show outside the playside tackle.

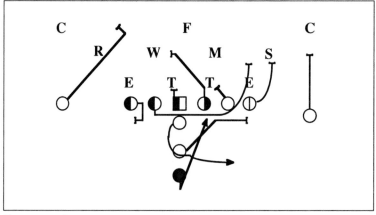

Figure 8-4. Power gap vs. 44

Figure 8-5 illustrates power gap versus 30 stack. The playside tight end gap blocks the 5 technique. The playside tackle posts the 5 technique before releasing for the Mike backer because the Mike backer is the second backer in the box. The playside guard gap blocks the 0 technique. The center posts the 0 technique before releasing for the backside backer because the backside guard is uncovered. The backside tackle executes a bubble cutoff. The fullback executes a kick-out block on the first defender to show outside the playside tackle.

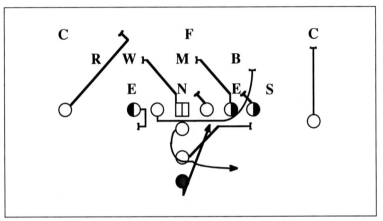

Figure 8-5. Power gap vs. 30 stack

Power gap may also be run to a trips formation when the defense plays zone coverage which forces one man out of the box to cover the slot receiver. The word *on* is added to enable the tight end to block the man on him if no lineman is inside him (Figure 8-6).

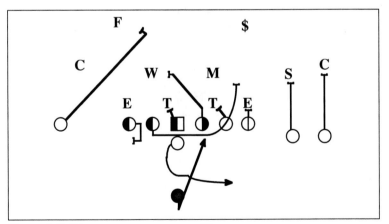

Figure 8-6. Trips, power gap on vs. 43 over

Counter Gap

When counter gap is the huddle call, the backside guard now becomes the kick-out blocker and the fullback pulls through the hole. All other assignments are the same as power gap. Figure 8-7 illustrates counter gap versus 43 over, and Figure 8-8 illustrates counter gap versus 43 under.

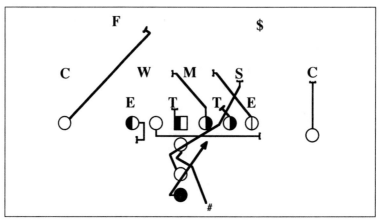

Figure 8-7. Counter gap vs. 43 over

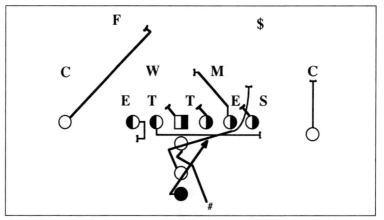

Figure 8-8. Counter gap vs. 43 under

Split End Side Power and Counter Gap

Power gap and counter gap can be run to the split end side by using the same "check with me" rule of two system that's used for one-back zone plays to the split end side. If two linebackers exist, counting from Mike to the force area, the play must be checked to the tight end side. Figure 8-9 illustrates power gap to the split end side versus 43 under. One way to avoid a second backer is to run gap scheme to a twins formation. Figure 8-10 illustrates counter gap to the twins side.

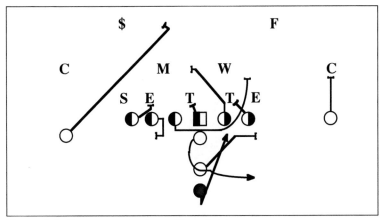

Figure 8-9. Power gap to the split end side

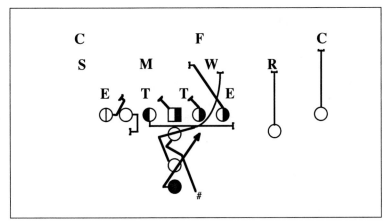

Figure 8-10. Twins, counter gap vs. 44

9

Other Plays and Other Schemes

It's tempting to run more plays and more schemes, and coaches can often find good reasons to do so. Plays and schemes that attack specific defensive adjustments or weaknesses and that just simply relate well to skills of athletes that a coach wishes to feature are legitimate reasons to add. A good analogy is to have a full toolbox so a coach can choose the wrench or screwdriver that fits.

However, not adding many more plays or schemes can be a good idea too. If players are confused about added assignments, they're also likely to blow assignments on base plays. More plays and schemes may also require different skills that must be practiced. Therefore, when a new play or scheme is added, a coach should consider subtracting something else from the playbook. The best course is if a new play can be blocked with the same schemes as other plays in the offense. When it's necessary to add a new blocking scheme, players should relate as close as possible to assignments and skills they're already learned.

Dive Option

A fullback dive and dive option are easy to add. The dive portion of the sequence can be blocked as tight zone, and the dive option can be blocked as wide zone (Figure 9-1).

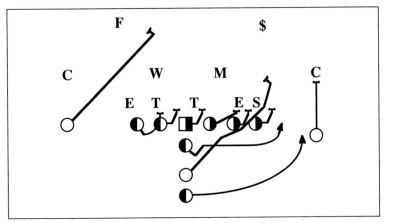

Figure 9-1. Dive option

Wide Zone Toss

- As in dive option, toss can be run with the wide zone scheme.
- Toss means *force*, so the playside tackle will call Tex instead of Ted if he's uncovered.
- The fullback will block the force player if one exists and will aim for the tackle's rear end and block the most dangerous player if no force player exists.

Figure 9-2 illustrates toss versus a 44 defense. The playside tackle calls *Tex*; he and the tight end will combo the man on the tight end to the first backer in the box. The playside guard's *cage* call can now work to the backside backer. The fullback blocks the force player.

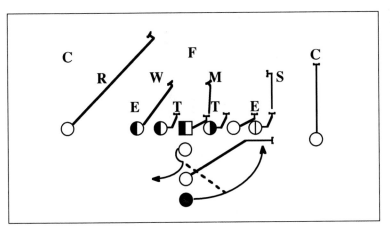

Figure 9-2. Toss vs. 44

Man Pull

- A man pull scheme can be installed as a change-up to wide zone blocking or it can be a substitute.
- The rule is simple: Playside covered linemen reach block the man on them and uncovered playside linemen pull for box linebackers.
- The center is playside if he's uncovered and backside if he's covered.
- Backside linemen scoop combo as they do in wide zone blocking.
- Covered playside linemen have the option of calling name tags when confronted by outside shades. The name tags are exchanges of assignment; the uncovered man blocks down and the covered man pulls. This technique is sometimes referred to as *pin and pull.*
- The fullback will block the force defender. If the play is run from one back, it should be run to trips so the force player can be blocked by the slot receiver.
- The play can be executed as a handoff or a toss.

Figure 9-3 illustrates man pull versus a 44 defense. The tight end and playside guard are covered and therefore, by rule, will reach block. The playside tackle is uncovered and by rule will pull for the first backer in the box, counting from outside in. In this case, the playside guard is covered by a 3 technique and has the option of calling *Tom.* Tom means the tackle will exchange assignments with the guard. The tackle will block the 3 technique, and the guard will pull for the backer. The center is uncovered and pulls for the Mike or first playside backer. If the playside backer is already blocked, as he would be in this case by the guard, the center will block the safety. The backside guard calls *uno* versus a backside 1 technique.

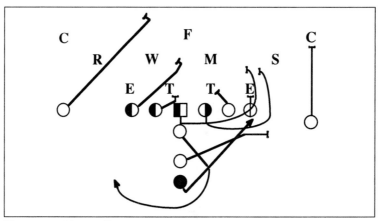

Figure 9-3. Man pull vs. 44

Figure 9-4 illustrates man pull versus 43 under. The tight end, playside tackle, and center are covered and by rule will reach block. In this case, the playside tackle is covered by a 5 technique and has the option of calling *Ed*. Ed means the tackle will exchange assignments with the tight end. The tight end will block the 5 technique, and the tackle will pull and block the 9 technique. The playside guard is uncovered and by rule will pull for the first playside backer. The center is covered by a 1 technique and has the option of calling *George*. George means the center will exchange assignments with the guard. The guard will block the 1 technique, and the center will pull for the backer. The backside guard calls *banjo*; he and the tackle scoop combo the 3 technique to the backside backer.

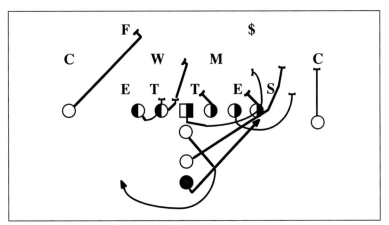

Figure 9-4. Man pull vs. 43 under

Isolation Play

- An isolation play is a man block scheme that could be run as a substitute for tight zone blast.
- The playside tight end will block the man on or outside. If the tackle calls *out*, the tight end will block the first defender outside.
- The playside tackle will block the man on. If uncovered, the tackle will call *out* to the tight end and will then block the first man outside. Versus a 43, the tackle will block the Sam backer.
- The playside guard will block the man on or will call *deuce* if he's uncovered. Deuce means that he and the center will combo the man on the center to the Mike or backside backer.
- The center will block the man on. If the playside guard calls *deuce*, the center and the guard will combo the man to the Mike or the backside backer.

- If the center is uncovered, he'll call *gut* and then block the backside A gap, as he does on gap scheme.
- The backside guard will block on or over. If the center calls *gut*, the guard will fold around the center's block and will block the backside backer.
- The backside tackle will block on. If the center calls *gut*, the tackle will bubble cutoff.
- The fullback will block the Mike or playside backer if the playside guard is covered, and will block the playside backer if the guard is uncovered.

Figure 9-5 illustrates isolation versus 43 under. The playside tackle and tight end block the 5 and 9 techniques, respectively. The playside guard calls *deuce* because he's uncovered; he and the center combo the 1 technique to the backside backer. The backside guard and tackle block the men on them. The fullback blocks the playside backer because the playside guard is uncovered.

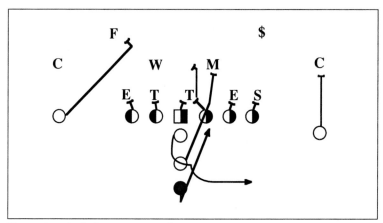

Figure 9-5. Isolation vs. 43 under

Figure 9-6 illustrates isolation versus a 44 defense. The playside tackle calls *out* because he's uncovered; he then blocks the 6 technique. The playside tight end blocks the outside backer because the tackle called *out*. The playside guard blocks the 3 technique. The center calls *gut* because he's uncovered; he then blocks the backside A gap. The backside guard fold blocks to the backside backer and the backside tackle executes a bubble cutoff. The fullback blocks the playside backer.

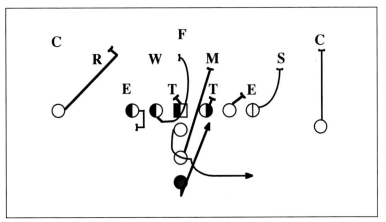

Figure 9-6. Isolation vs. 44

Trap

- Trap is a finesse play that's best run when backers play deep and is most effective if checked to a 3 technique.
- The playside tight end will block the first playside backer when the tackle is covered and will block the second backer, counting from Mike, when the tackle is uncovered.
- The playside tackle will block the Mike backer or the first playside backer. Versus a 30 stack, the tackle will block through the B gap to the most dangerous backer.
- If the center calls *deuce*, the playside guard will combo the 0 or 1 technique to the Mike or backside backer. If the center calls *Charlie*, the playside guard will pass set and block the first outside.
- If the center is covered, he'll call *deuce*, which means that he and the playside guard will combo the 0 or 1 technique to the Mike or backside backer. If the center is uncovered, he'll call *Charlie* and then block the first backside lineman.
- The backside guard will trap the first unblocked man past the center.
- If the center calls *deuce*, the backside tackle will block the guard's area or will block through the B gap to the backside backer. If the center calls *Charlie*, the backside tackle will block through the B gap to the backside backer.

Figure 9-7 illustrates trap vs. 43 under. The tight end blocks the first playside backer because the tackle is covered. The playside tackle blocks the playside backer. The center calls *deuce* because he's covered; he and the playside guard combo the 1 technique to the backside backer. The backside guard traps the playside 5 technique because he's the first unblocked man past the center. The backside tackle blocks the backside guard's area because the center called deuce.

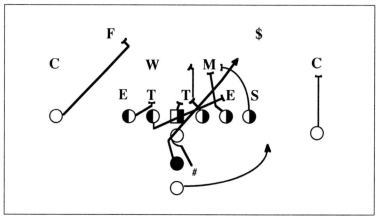

Figure 9-7. Trap vs. 43 under

Figure 9-8 illustrates trap versus 43 over. The tight end blocks the second backer, counting from Mike, because the tackle is uncovered. The playside tackle blocks the Mike backer. The playside guard pass sets and blocks the first outside because the center is uncovered. The center calls *Charlie* because he's uncovered; he then blocks the first backside lineman. The backside guard traps the playside 3 technique because he's the first unblocked man past the center. The backside tackle blocks the backside backer because the center called *Charlie*.

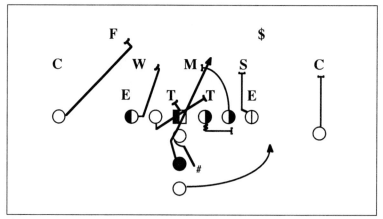

Figure 9-8. Trap vs. 43 over

Dart Counter

- Dart is a counter play run to the split end side only and can be run as a substitute to counter gap.
- The playside tackle will pass set and block the second defensive lineman. If only one defensive lineman exists, the tackle will block him.
- The playside guard will block the first defensive lineman; if he's on the tackle, the guard will pass set before blocking him. If only one defensive lineman exists, the guard will pass set and release for the second backside backer.
- The center and backside guard will block as if they're playside in tight zone.
- The center will block the man on or respond to the backside guard's cage call.
- The backside guard will block as if he's playside in tight zone. If covered, he'll call *cage*. If uncovered, he'll call *tag*.
- The backside tackle will pull to the playside through the first daylight to the most dangerous backer.
- The backside tight end will block the C gap.

Figure 9-9 illustrates dart versus 43 over. The playside tackle blocks the 5 technique because he's the second defensive lineman. The playside guard blocks the 1 technique because he's the first defensive lineman. The center and the backside guard execute a cage combo on the 3 technique to the Mike backer. The backside tackle pulls and blocks the playside backer, and the backside tight end blocks the backside C gap.

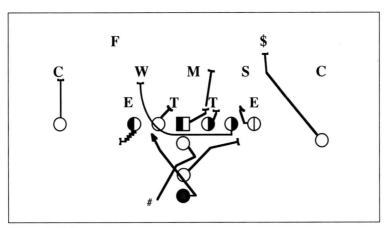

Figure 9-9. Dart vs. 43 over

Figure 9-10 illustrates dart versus 43 under. The playside tackle blocks the 5 technique because he's the second defensive lineman. The playside guard blocks the 3 technique because he's the first defensive lineman. The center blocks the backside 1 technique. The backside guard executes a tag combo on the 5 technique to the Mike backer. The backside tackle pulls and blocks the playside backer, and the backside tight end blocks the backside C gap.

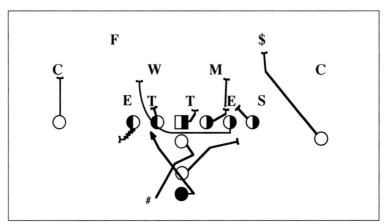

Figure 9-10. Dart vs. 43 under

10

Play-Action Pass Protections

Five play-action protection schemes are used in this system. The first of these is identical to the five-step drop protection but with a more aggressive approach on the playside. It's referred to as *fan* and is given the number of the run play, which the players fake. This protection allows three or more receivers into the route, with the fourth and fifth out being the backs who may check-release after the run fake and after they've checked off on their blitz responsibilities.

- The playside guard and tackle are assigned to specific defenders, and the center, backside guard, and backside tackle are assigned to block the backside A, B, and C gaps, respectively.
- The playside tackle will block the second defensive lineman. If the guard calls *squeeze*, the tackle will block the first defensive lineman outside the A gap.
- The playside guard will block the first defensive lineman and call *squeeze* versus a 0 technique or an A gap walkup backer. If the guard calls squeeze, he will slide to the A gap and block the 0 technique if he rushes playside or check-blitzes if he rushes backside. The guard will block the A gap walkup backer.
- The center will block the backside 1 technique or turn back to block the backside A gap. If nothing shows, the center will help backside.

- The backside guard will turn back and block the backside B gap. If nothing shows, the guard will help backside.
- The backside tackle will turn back and block the backside C gap.
- The tailback will come off the fake and block the Mike or first playside backer if he blitzes playside.
- The fullback will block the second playside backer, counting from Mike, if he blitzes playside.

Figure 10-1 illustrates fan protection versus 43 over, and Figure 10-2 illustrates fan protection versus 43 under. When fan protection is used from a one-back formation, the tailback has a double-read; he must block the Mike or first playside backer if he blitzes playside and then block the second playside backer if the first backer doesn't blitz (Figure 10-3).

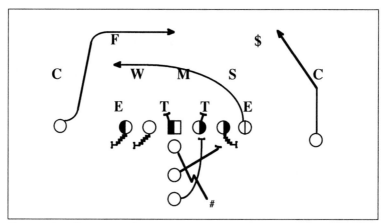

Figure 10-1. Fan protection vs. 43 over

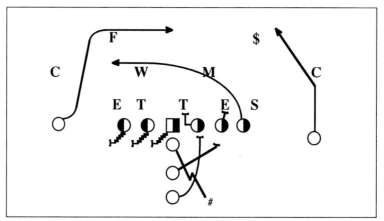

Figure 10-2. Fan protection vs. 43 under

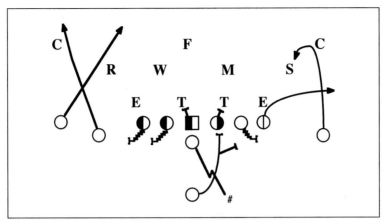

Figure 10-3. One-back fan protection vs. 44

Fan protection and the five-step drop protection are practiced in a live drill called *lover's lane*. The drill is set up in two segments. The first segment consists of the playside guard and tackle versus a defensive tackle and defensive end. The defensive alignments are practiced against simulated 43 over (Figure 10-4) and 43 under (Figure 10-5). Variety can be added to the drill by having the two defensive linemen execute twist stunts, in which case the two offensive lineman switch off.

Figure 10-4. Playside lover's lane vs. 43 over

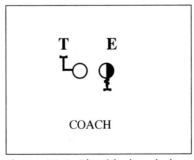

Figure 10-5. Playside lover's lane vs. 43 under

The second segment of the drill consists of the center, backside guard, and backside tackle versus a defensive tackle, defensive end, and backside linebacker. As in the playside segment, the alignments are practiced against simulated 43 over (Figure 10-6) and 43 under (Figure 10-7). In this case all players turn back and block whatever shows up in their gaps. If no one shows up, they help to their outside. A variety of blitzes by the backer are included.

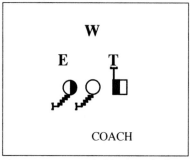

Figure 10-6. Backside lover's lane vs. 43 over

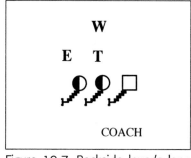

Figure 10-7. Backside lover's lane vs. 43 under

The second protection used is given the run number with the word *pass* attached.

- The tailback has no blitz responsibility, and the fullback or a backside tight end must block backside.
- Because the playside tight end is needed to block the D gap, only two receivers are in the route, with the possibility of the tailback as a checkdown receiver.
- All linemen will reach into their playside gap and block any threat. If no threat appears, the linemen will pivot on their playside feet and block any backside threats.

Figures 10-8, 10-9, and 10-10 illustrate three plays that may be faked with this protection.

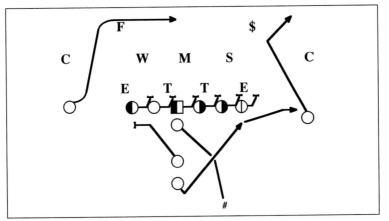

Figure 10-8. Wide zone pass protection

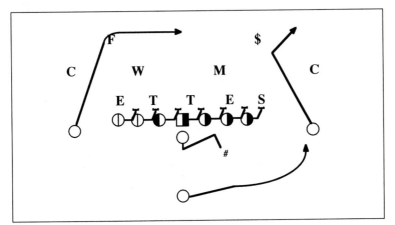

Figure 10-9. Option pass protection

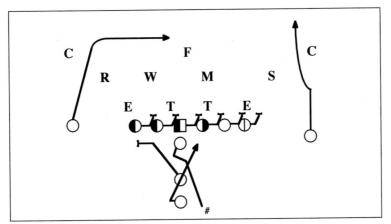

Figure 10-10. Counter pass protection

The third protection is given the run number with the word *bootleg left* or *bootleg right* attached. Figure 10-11 illustrates bootleg protection.

- If the tight end is playside, he'll attack his inside gap. If he's backside, he'll run a drag pattern.
- Playside linemen and the center will attack their inside or backside gaps.
- The backside guard will pull flat for three steps, open his hips, and work to 4 yards deep while identifying his target. His target is the first to show outside the end man on the line of scrimmage.
- If the target isn't as deep as the guard, he should continue outside and block his outside number. If he's as deep as the guard, he should kick him out. If he disappears inside with the fake, the guard should continue outside, with his head on a swivel.
- The backside tackle will slide to the B gap and then turn back if no threat appears.
- The tailback blocks the C gap after taking his fake.

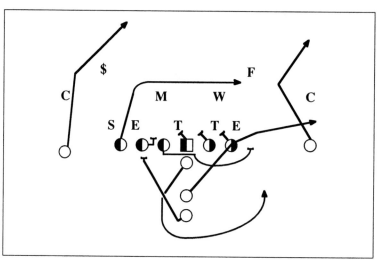

Figure 10-11. Bootleg protection

The fourth protection is given a play number with the name *roll* attached. Roll protection is identical to bootleg protection, with the exception that no direction is given. Playside will now be indicated by the play number. Figure 10-12 illustrates roll protection.

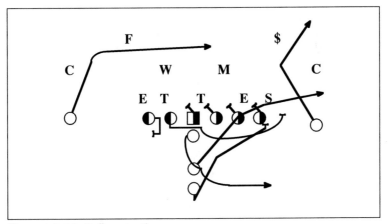

Figure 10-12. Roll protection

The final protection is called *naked* and is again attached to the run number being faked. All linemen will pull step two steps to the direction of the run number given and will block whatever crosses their faces. The fullback will ensure the backside C gap and will release if the C gap rusher is chasing inside. Figure 10-13 illustrates naked protection.

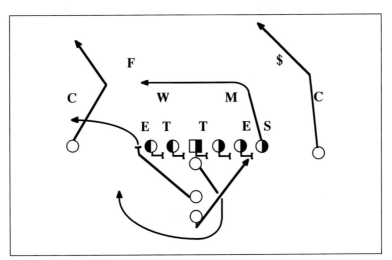

Figure 10-13. Naked protection

In addition to play-action passes, this system has two play-action screens: wide zone screen and naked screen. Figure 10-14 illustrates wide zone screen. The playside guard and tackle block wide zone pass rules for two counts before releasing to the screen area. All other linemen execute wide zone pass away from the play. Figure 10-15 illustrates naked screen. The playside guard and tackle block backside naked technique for two counts before releasing to the screen area. All other linemen execute naked technique to the side of the play.

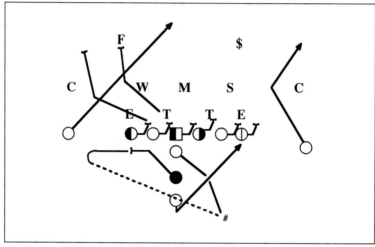

Figure 10-14. Wide zone screen

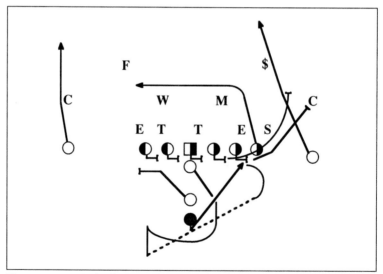

Figure 10-15. Naked screen

11

Short-Yardage Offense

When a team has 3 yards or fewer to be gained, the following run plays can be used:
- Wide zone force
- Tight zone blast
- Option load
- Power gap
- Fullback wedge

Wide Zone Force

Figure 11-1 illustrates wide zone force versus 65 goal line. The fullback blocks the strong safety because he's the force player. The wingback blocks the corner. The playside guard calls *tag* versus a 65 look; he and the tackle combo the 5 technique to the first playside backer. The playside tight end blocks the 9 technique. The center blocks the playside gap. The backside guard calls *uno* versus a 65 look. The backside tackle blocks the backside backer, and the backside tight end blocks the 5 technique because he's the third defender.

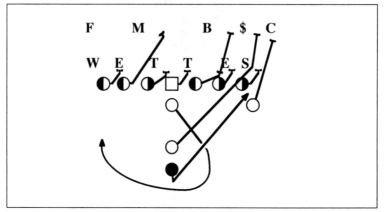

Figure 11-1. Wide zone force vs. 65 goal line

Figure 11-2 illustrates wide zone force versus 56 goal line. The fullback blocks the strong safety because he's the force player. The wingback blocks the corner. The playside tackle calls *Tex* because he's uncovered; he and the tight end combo the 6 technique to the first backer in the box. The playside guard calls *cage* because he's covered; he and the center combo the 3 technique to the Mike backer. The center calls *Eagle* because he and the playside guard are covered. The backside guard blocks the 0 technique, and the backside tackle blocks the guard's area because the center called *Eagle*. The backside tight end blocks the 6 technique because he's the third defender.

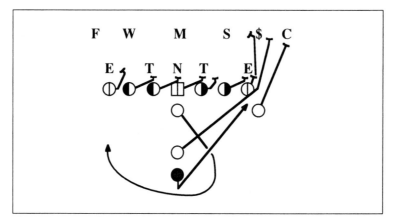

Figure 11-2. Wide zone force vs. 56 goal line

Tight Zone Blast

Figure 11-3 illustrates tight zone blast versus 65 goal line. The fullback blocks the playside backer. The wingback blocks the force player. The playside guard calls *ace*; he and the center combo the A gap player to the backside backer. The playside tight end and tackle block the 5 and 9 techniques, respectively. The backside guard calls *uno* versus a 65 look. The backside tackle blocks the backside backer, and the backside tight end blocks the 5 technique because he's the third defender.

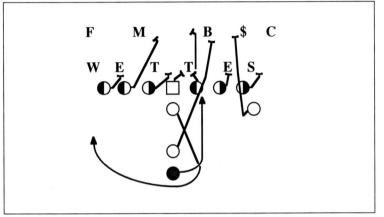

Figure 11-3. Tight zone blast vs. 65 goal line

Figure 11-4 illustrates tight zone blast versus 56 goal line. The fullback blocks the playside backer. The wingback blocks the force player. The playside tackle calls *Ted* because he's uncovered; he and the tight end combo the 6 technique to the Sam backer because he's the second playside backer, counting from the Mike backer. The playside guard calls *cage* because he's covered; he and the center combo the 3 technique to the Mike backer. The center calls *Eagle* because he and the playside guard are covered. The backside guard blocks the 0 technique and the backside tackle blocks the guard's area because the center called *Eagle*. The backside tight end blocks the 6 technique because he's the third defender.

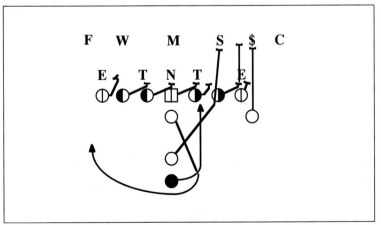

Figure 11-4. Tight zone blast vs. 56 goal line

Option Load

When the option is run in short yardage, option load should be called rather than option seal. The playside tight end will block a 9 technique, and the fullback will lead through the C gap. The quarterback will option the first defender to show outside the tight end's block but will cut into the C gap if the 9 technique widens. The reason this scheme is used versus short yardage defenses is because of the possibility of a quarterback/pitchback responsibility exchange between the 9 technique and the defensive back who's playing right behind him. For example, if the 9 technique were to take the pitchback, it would give the quarterback a keep read and deliver him right into the waiting arms of the defensive back. In the load scheme, the fullback will lead into the C gap, thus ensuring the quarterback keeps dimension of the option.

Figure 11-5 illustrates option load versus 65 goal line. The tight end blocks the 9 technique and the fullback blocks through the C gap. The playside guard calls *tag* versus a 65 look; he and the tackle combo the 5 technique to the Mike backer because he's the first playside backer. The center blocks the playside gap. The backside guard calls *uno* versus a 65 look and the backside tackle blocks the backside backer. The backside tight end blocks the 5 technique because he's the third defender.

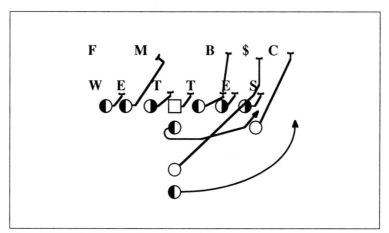

Figure 11-5. Option load vs. 65 goal line

Figure 11-6 illustrates option load versus 56 goal line. The fullback blocks through the C gap. The playside tackle calls *Tex* because he's uncovered; he and the tight end combo the 6 technique to the Sam backer because he's the first backer in the box. The playside guard calls *cage* because he's covered; he and the center combo the 3 technique to the Mike backer. The center calls *Eagle* because he and the playside guard are covered. The backside guard blocks the 0 technique and the backside tackle

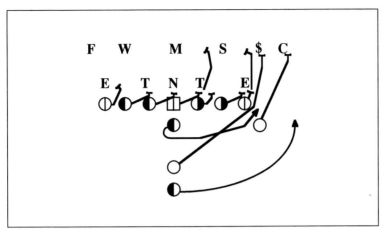

Figure 11-6. Option load vs. 56 goal line

blocks the guard's area because the center called *Eagle*. The backside tight end blocks the 6 technique because he's the third defender.

Power Gap

Figure 11-7 illustrates power gap versus 65 goal line. The wingback executes a kick-out block on the 9 technique. The fullback leads through the hole. The tight end gap blocks the 5 technique. The playside tackle post blocks the 5 technique before releasing for the backside backer. The playside guard blocks the A gap player. The center blocks the backside A gap player. The backside guard pulls through the hole for the playside backer. The backside tackle executes a bubble cutoff, and the backside tight end blocks the 5 technique because he's the third defender.

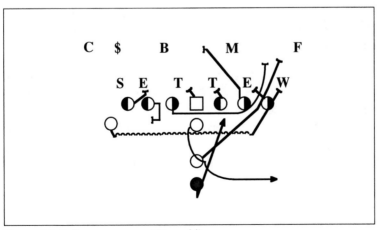

Figure 11-7. Power gap vs. 65 goal line

Figure 11-8 illustrates power gap versus 56 goal line. The wingback executes a kick-out block on the 6 technique. The fullback leads through the hole. The tight end releases outside when no inside lineman exists. The playside tackle gap blocks the 3 technique. The playside guard gap blocks the 0 technique. The center blocks the backside A gap because the backside guard is covered. The backside guard pulls through the hole to the Mike backer, and the backside tackle executes a bubble cutoff. The backside tight end blocks the 6 technique because he's the third defender.

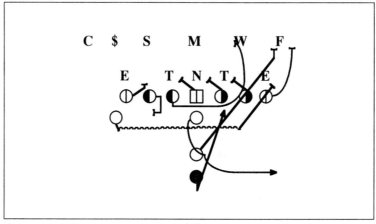

Figure 11-8. Power gap vs. 56 goal line

Fullback Wedge

The fullback wedge is the final play in the short yardage package. The apex of the wedge is the playside guard. Versus a 65, the guard will call *A*, which tells the center to double the A gap defender with the guard. Versus a 56, the guard will call *B*, which tells the tackle to double the B gap defender with the guard. All other playside linemen will block their inside gaps, scramble blocking any lineman who may be in that gap. Backside linemen block zone rules.

Figure 11-9 illustrates fullback wedge versus 65 goal line. The playside guard calls *A* because an A gap defender exists; he and the center double-team the A gap. The playside tackle blocks through the B gap to the Mike backer. The playside tight end scramble blocks the 5 technique because he's in the C gap. The backside guard calls *uno* versus a 65 look, and the backside tackle blocks the backside backer. The backside tight end blocks the 5 technique because he's the third defender.

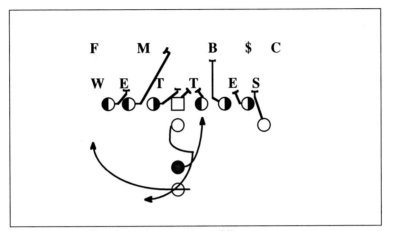

Figure 11-9. Fullback wedge vs. 65 goal line

Figure 11-10 illustrates fullback wedge versus 56 goal line. The playside guard calls *B* because a B gap defender exists. The playside tight end blocks through the C gap to the playside backer. The backside guard calls *smash* because a 0 technique is being played on the center; he and the center combo the 0 technique to the Mike backer. The backside tackle blocks the backside 3 technique because he's the first backside lineman. The backside tight end blocks the 6 technique.

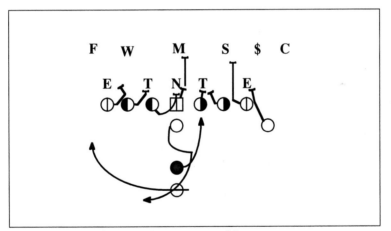

Figure 11-10. Fullback wedge vs. 56 goal line

Short-Yardage Play-Action Protections

The following five play-action passes are used in the short-yardage package:

- Fan (Figure 11-11)
- Option load pass (Figure 11-12)
- Roll (Figure 11-13)
- Bootleg (Figure 11-14)
- Naked (Figure 11-15)

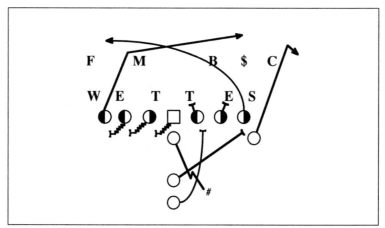

Figure 11-11. Fan protection

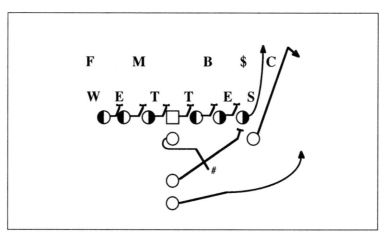

Figure 11-12. Option load pass protection

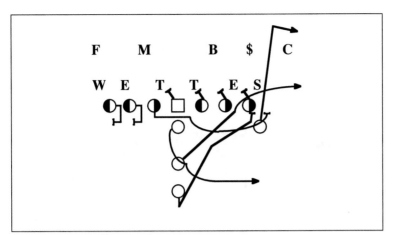

Figure 11-13. Roll protection

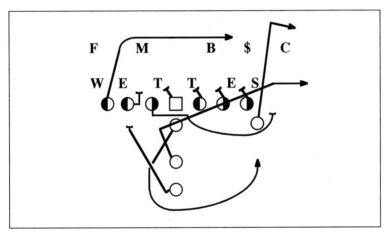

Figure 11-14. Bootleg protection

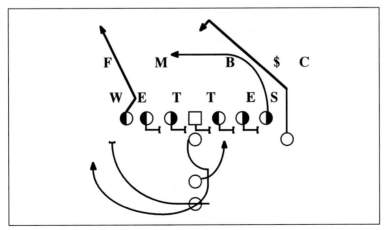

Figure 11-15. Naked protection

12

Adapting the System to Other Offenses

When a coach builds his run game around blocking schemes rather than building blocking schemes to fit plays, he'll have a blocking system that can be adapted to virtually any offensive approach.

Shotgun Spread Option Offense

The shotgun spread option is currently a popular trend and can be used to supplement the run game detailed in this book or it can be a system in itself. In either case, the zone and gap schemes can be incorporated. Figure 12-1 illustrates the base play in

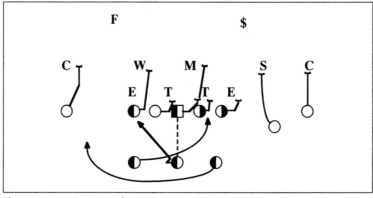

Figure 12-1. Zone read

the spread option—the tight zone read—in which the quarterback "reads" the backside defensive end. The quarterback will complete the handoff to the running back if the defensive end plays soft for the quarterback keep or will pull the ball and keep it if the defensive end chases the zone play to the running back. A one-back shotgun has no pitch dimension.

Figure 12-2 illustrates fly sweep incorporating wide zone blocking. The running back would block a force player or ensure pursuit from inside if no force player exists. A wide zone play can also be executed by the running back or by the quarterback, with the running back as a lead blocker. Figure 12-3 illustrates the companion play to the fly sweep: the quarterback power gap. Power gap can also be executed by a running back in a two-back shotgun, with the other back being the kick-out blocker. Figure 12-4 illustrates option seal to a split end side from a one-back shotgun formation. The play could also be run to the tight end side.

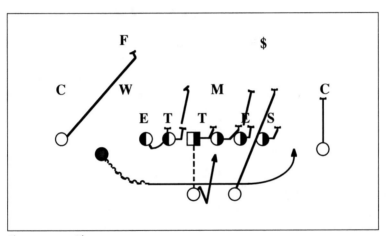

Figure 12-2. Fly sweep

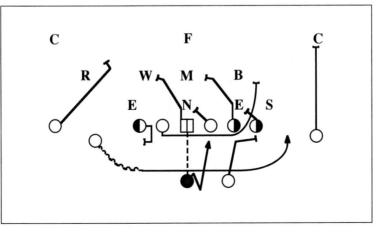

Figure 12-3. Quarterback power gap

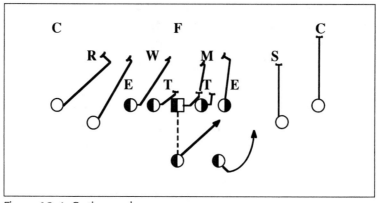

Figure 12-4. Option seal

Wing-T Offense

The wing-T offense is a three-back formation, with one of the halfbacks aligned as a wingback and the other as a dive back. Plays to the strongside feature the wingback as a blocker or counter threat. All these plays can be mirrored to the weakside when the wingback uses short motion to place him in a dive back position at the snap of the ball. The dive back would now be the blocker or counter threat. The fullback provides the inside threat or is an additional lead blocker.

Figure 12-5 illustrates wide zone blocking being used to run the power sweep. The wingback will help the tight end if needed or seal the inside pursuit. Figure 12-6 illustrates tight zone blocking being used to run the fullback belly play. A belly option play would use wide zone blocking. Figure 12-7 illustrates gap blocking being used to run the power gap play. Figure 12-8 illustrates gap blocking being used to run the wingback counter play, with the backside tight end pulling through the hole.

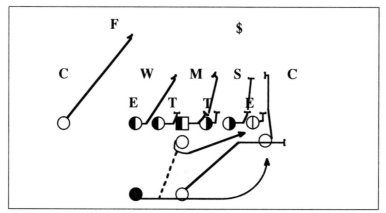

Figure 12-5. Power sweep

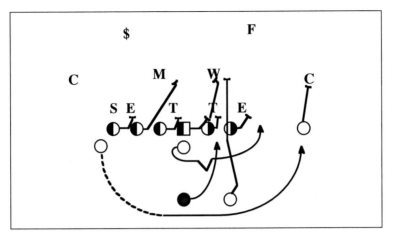

Figure 12-6. Fullback belly

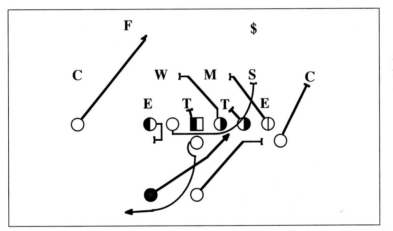

Figure 12-7. Power gap

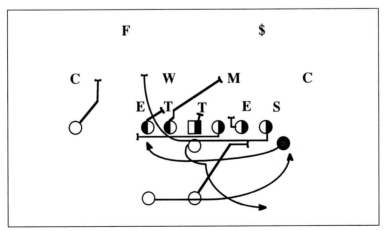

Figure 12-8. Wingback counter

Triple Option Offense

The triple option offense is another three-back offense, tracing its roots to the wishbone and split back veer offenses. The inside dimension is the fullback, with the two slotbacks playing the roles of pitchback or lead blocker. The predetermined dive and option would be run with tight and wide zone blocking, respectively. The triple option would be run with adjustments to wide zone blocking by attaching the word *veer* to the play call.

- Veer means that the quarterback will execute a give/keep read on the defensive line defender who aligns on or outside the playside tackle.
- The playside guard will call *veer* when he's covered or versus a playside 1 technique. Veer means that the center playside guard and playside tackle are involved in a three-man zone to block the A and B gaps to the playside backer. The guard blocks the first playside lineman, the center blocks through the A gap to the playside backer, and the tackle blocks through the B gap to the playside backer.
- When the guard is uncovered, he'll call *tag*. The handoff key versus a 30 is the first defensive lineman, and he's blocked as in wide zone with a tag combo. The quarterback will now read the reaction of the handoff key to the zone combo to determine give or keep.
- The playside slotback will arc block on the force player versus a two-safety coverage and will seal on the playside backer versus a one-safety coverage.

Figure 12-9 illustrates triple option versus 43, cover 2. The playside guard calls *veer* because he's covered; he then blocks the man on. The playside tackle blocks through the B gap to the first playside backer. The center blocks through the A gap to the playside backer. The backside guard calls *banjo*; he and the backside tackle scoop combo the 2 technique to the backside backer. The playside slotback arc blocks on the defensive force because two safeties exist. The quarterback's give/keep read is the defensive end, and his keep/pitch read is the Sam backer.

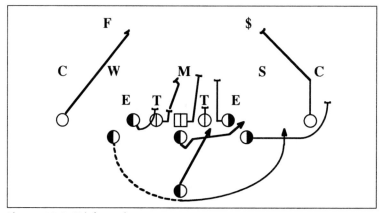

Figure 12-9. Triple option vs. 43, cover 2

Figure 12-10 illustrates triple option versus 44, cover 3. The playside guard calls *veer* because he's covered; he then blocks the man on. The playside tackle blocks through the B gap to the first playside backer. The center blocks through the A gap to the playside backer. The backside guard calls *banjo*; he and the backside tackle scoop combo the 2 technique to the backside backer. The playside slotback will seal the scraping playside backer because only one safety exists. The quarterback's give/keep read is the defensive end, and his keep/pitch read is the Sam backer.

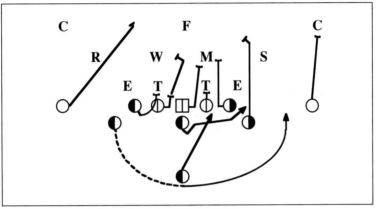

Figure 12-10. Triple option vs. 44, cover 3

Figure 12-11 illustrates triple option versus 34, cover 2. The playside guard calls *tag* because he's uncovered; he and the tackle execute a *tag* combo on the 5 technique to the playside backer. The backside guard calls *smash* versus a 0 technique; he and the center scoop combo the 0 technique to the backside backer. The backside tackle blocks the 5 technique because he's the first backside lineman. The playside slot arc blocks the defensive force player because two safeties exist. The quarterback will read the combo versus any 30 alignment for his give/keep read. The keep/pitch read is the Sam backer.

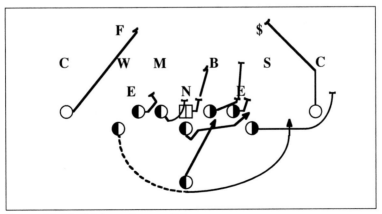

Figure 12-11. Triple option vs. 34, cover

The gap scheme can used to block the counter option play. Figure 12-12 illustrates counter option versus a 44 defense. The playside slotback load blocks the defensive end. The playside tackle gap blocks the 2 technique. The playside guard post blocks the 2 technique before releasing for the backside backer. The center blocks the backside A gap. The backside tackle executes a bubble cutoff. The backside pulling guard pulls around the slotback's block for the playside backer. The quarterback options the next defender to show outside.

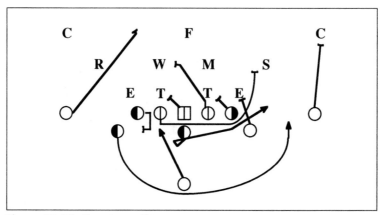

Figure 12-12. Counter option

About the Author

John Rose is currently retired after teaching high school social studies and coaching high school football for more than 30 years at Adair-Casey High School (1969 to 1976) in Adair, Iowa, and Creston High School (1976 to 2004) in Creston, Iowa. In addition, he served for one year (1980 to 1981) as an American exchange teacher at Bosworth College in Desford, England, where he learned to appreciate the contributions of rugby to the evolution of American football.

Rose's total coaching experience includes coaching the offensive line, offensive backs, linebackers, and defensive backs as well as serving as defensive coordinator. Over the years, players coached by Rose and other members of the Creston Orient-Macksburg staff have played at the University of Iowa, Iowa State University, Drake University, Southwest Missouri State University, Northeast Missouri State University, Northwest Missouri State University, Buena Vista (Iowa) University, St. John's (Minnesota) University, St. Ambrose (Iowa) University, William Penn (Iowa) University, Wartburg (Iowa) College, Central (Iowa) College, and Simpson (Iowa) College as well as at a number of community colleges, with one player being invited to participate in pre-season camp by the New York Jets.

Rose received his bachelor's degree in history and political science in 1969 and his master's degree in social studies curriculum in 1975 from Mankato State University (now known as Minnesota State).

Rose and his wife, Lois, enjoy visiting their grandchildren, traveling, attending Iowa Hawkeyes football games, attending musicals and plays at the Des Moines Civic Center, fishing, and pheasant hunting with their springer spaniel named Molly.